THOMSON-SHORE

Helping you put your best book forward

Thomson-Shore, Inc. | 7300 West Joy Road | Dexter, MI 48130-9701
Ph: 734-426-3034 | Fax: 734-426-6219 | www.thomsonshore.com

RIVER MUSIC

BINDING	Case Bound
PAGES	224
TEXT	Natures Book Natural 30% PCR FSC MIXED 60# 50x38 Black ink
CLOTH	54" Pearl Linen 54160 Forest Pine (L)

*** SAMPLE BOOK *** NOT FOR RESALE ***

JACKET	Litho Label Gloss C1S 100# 4 color process Scuff Resistant Layflat Matte Lamination
FOILStamp S	S20 Satin Gold 24"

*** SAMPLE BOOK *** NOT FOR RESALE ***

River Music

NUMBER TWENTY
Gulf Coast Books
Sponsored by Texas A&M University–Corpus Christi
John W. Tunnell Jr., General Editor

A list of other titles in this series appears at the back of the book.

River Music

An Atchafalaya Story

ANN McCUTCHAN

Texas A&M University Press | College Station

LIBRARY OF CONGRESS CATALOGING-IN-PUBLICATION DATA

McCutchan, Ann.
  River music : an Atchafalaya story / Ann McCutchan. — 1st ed.
    p. cm. — (Gulf Coast books ; no. 20)
  Includes bibliographical references and index.
  ISBN-13: 978-1-60344-289-3 (cloth : alk. paper)
  ISBN-10: 1-60344-289-8 (cloth : alk. paper)
  ISBN-13: 978-1-60344-322-7 (e-book)
  ISBN-10: 1-60344-322-3 (e-book)
  1. Robicheaux, Earl, 1954-   2. Composers—Louisiana—
Atchafalaya River Region—Biography.   3. Atchafalaya River
Region (La.)—Biography.   4. Atchafalaya River Region (La.)—
Environmental conditions.   5. Nature sounds—Recording and
reproducing—Louisiana—Atchafalaya River Region.
6. Soundscapes (Music)—Louisiana—Atchafalaya
River Region—History and criticism.
I. Title.   II. Series: Gulf Coast books ; no. 20.
F377.A78M33   2011
976.3'4—dc22
2010054351

*Jacket, title page, and dedication page art by Pat Alexander, from the
Atchafalaya series, 2006–07, oil on panel.*

Chapter heading photographs by Pat Alexander and Ann McCutchan.

This book is dedicated
to the memory of
my maternal grandfather,
Horace Bond,
consummate outdoorsman
and early conservationist,
who in the 1930s led a
successful campaign to clean up
the Penobscot River in Maine.
Thanks to Grandfather,
the paper mills stopped
dumping refuse in the river,
and the salmon, which had
ceased spawning there,
returned.

When I go into the swamps,
I feel like I'm in another world.
I feel closer to God.
I can talk to God better,
you know?
No interruptions.

—Adam Morales, fisherman,
driftwood sculpture artist,
Pierre Part
Atchafalaya River Basin
Louisiana

Contents

Preface

The Atchafalaya River Basin has fascinated me since the 1970s, when I lived as a marginally employed musician in New Orleans and, during my many off-hours, explored south Louisiana's rich natural environment and diverse culture. When I left the state for better work, I merely crossed over into Texas, and though I've lived in other places since, I've mostly resided within a day's drive of the Atchafalaya, the heartland of Acadiana and North America's largest rain forest. Somehow, the region has always called to me.

In time, I found reasons to write about the Atchafalaya—in a piece of travel literature, in a lyric text for a musical composition. But early in 2005, I felt compelled to try something more substantial, and the idea was inspired by the memory of an old friend, south Louisiana musician and naturalist Earl Robicheaux, who had some years before introduced me to the natural sound sources in the basin's bayous, swamps, fields, and forests. I would need help with a large, as yet unformed project, and I knew Earl would be willing to assist me, if I could track him down.

But as is usual for me, I allowed the idea to float for a while, and it was not until late August, when Hurricane Katrina hit, that I got to work looking for Earl. I was frightened, then. What if he lived in the storm's path? What if he hadn't evacuated in time?

As it turned out, Earl had a ringside seat for Katrina, watching it tear into New Orleans from an ICU unit in Charity Hospital, where he had just begun treatment for Burkitt's lymphoma. By the time I drove down from North Texas to visit him, he had been airlifted from Charity's roof and set down in Baton Rouge General. There, hooked up to a bank of bleeping monitors, my friend caught me up on his activities: how in the intervening years he had made it his life's work to document the birds, animals, weather, and other sonic phenomena in the Atchafalaya through archival recordings and original soundscapes—compositions created from environmental sounds. He was worried about the basin's hydrological system, he said. Crippled over the years by damming, dredging, and other attempts to control them for expedient commercial use, the basin's originally graceful, looping rivers, lakes, and bayous were undergoing problems like increased sedimentation and poor water quality. Earl wanted to capture his native environment before it disappeared, and I, understanding he might not live to accomplish his goals, tuned into his urgency, completing the calling to write.

And so, I began to devote my free time to exploring the Atchafalaya Basin with Earl, with others, and by myself. I spoke to people, read books, took photographs, scratched notes. I wandered around by car, by boat, on foot. And after two years, I had enough background and information to begin a book, but no organizing experience for it. I was not from south Louisiana, nor was I a scientist or certified naturalist. Maybe, I thought, my "call" was a hoax.

Then one day in spring 2007, I read to a writing class a scene I'd drafted that happened to feature Earl. It was a good choice. Earl is a fine storyteller, as so many south Louisianans are, with a flair for both the poetic and the absurd. And, as a Cajun man who nearly established a sophisticated musical life outside Louisiana, and through a series of unlikely events, found a purpose in his home territory, his personal tale appeals.

When I finished reading, I invited questions, and a girl named Amber raised her hand. "Will Earl be present throughout the book?" she asked, as if her further interest depended on it.

Struck by the brilliant idea in her question, I answered, "Yes," as if I'd intended to do it from the start. That night, I called Earl. "Would it be OK if I use your life to tell a story about the basin?" I asked. "Would you be comfortable as a main character?"

"Sure," he replied.

While I was relieved to secure a dual focus—a person as well as a place—I now had to encounter the challenges inherent in writing about a friend. We all weave myths about ourselves, and Earl admits he is no exception. Though he laughs when he describes his life as "epic," he does see some events on that scale, likening himself to a character in a novel—and maybe, in the end, he is that kind of character. It is no wonder then that I, the chronicler hoping for an attractive arc, found myself lured by my friend's self-narrative. Well, why not turn on the tape recorder, let Earl talk, and pour it onto some pages? But I knew the limits of unaccompanied solos and saw that Earl's story deserved a chorus of voices in counterpoint, as did the Atchafalaya's. So, while my friendship with Earl and his experiences drive this book, so does input from more than sixty other individuals, including friends from all stages of Earl's life, relatives, teachers, professional colleagues, Atchafalaya area residents, and experts on basin ecology. Rounding out the choir are some of the men and women of the Atchafalaya Earl interviewed for oral history projects commissioned by state agencies. I was fortunate enough to be given access to the tapes before they were archived.

Acknowledgments

Besides Earl, I have plenty of people to thank, chief among them the individuals I interviewed for this book. Though I did not quote them all, every one contributed invaluably to the whole. They include Frédéric Allamel, art sociologist and educator, Indianapolis; John Amrhein, photographer, Berlin; C. Ray Brassieur, University of Louisiana, Lafayette, Department of Sociology and Anthropology; David Burke, Fulton County, Ga.; Mike Carloss, assistant chief, Louisiana Department of Wildlife and Fisheries, Baton Rouge; Charles Chamberlain, museum historian, Louisiana State Museum, New Orleans; Stephen Chustz, acting director, Louisiana Department of Natural Resources, Atchafalaya Basin Program, Baton Rouge; Sherbin Collette, commercial fisherman and mayor of Henderson, La.; Miriam Davey, naturalist, Baton Rouge; Paul Davidson, executive director, Black Bear Conservation Coalition, Baton Rouge; Jim Delahoussaye, biologist, US Department of Environmental Quality (retired), Butte La Rose, La.; Charles Demas, director, US Geological Survey, Louisiana Water Science Center, Baton Rouge; Hanns Berthold Dietz, professor emeritus, musicology, University of Texas, Austin; Steve DiMarco, Department of Oceanography, Texas A&M University, College Station; Randall Dooley, Patterson, La.; James Mulcro Drew, composer, New York/Amsterdam; Bill Fontenot, naturalist and writer, Carencro, La.; Greg Guirard, commercial fisherman, photographer, and author, St. Martinville, La.; Lamar Hale, project manager, Army Corps of Engineers, New Orleans; Karl Korte, composer and professor of composition (retired), University of Texas, Austin; Carolyn Robicheaux Larive, Berwick, La.; Cassidy LeJeune, biologist supervisor, Louisiana Department of Wildlife and Fisheries, New Iberia; Rudy Malveaux, Austin, Tex.; Stephen Montague, composer, London; Pauline Oliveros, composer, Kingston, N.Y.; Riki Ott, community activist and *Exxon Valdez* oil spill expert, Cordova, Ak.; Scott Ramsey, attorney and landowner, Morgan City, La.; Vickie L. Robertson, Hitchcock, Tex.; Eula Thibodeaux Robicheaux, Berwick, La.; Gwen Roland, author of *Atchafalaya Houseboat: My Years in the Louisiana Swamp* (LSU Press), Pike County, Ga.; Stacey Scarce, naturalist, outdoor guide, and manager, Acadiana Park Nature Station, Lafayette; Wilma Subra, chemist, environmental activist, and MacArthur Fellow, New Iberia; Rose Thibodaux, Lafayette; Wes Tunnell, biologist and associate director of the Harte Research Institute for Gulf of Mexico Studies (Texas A&M University–Corpus Christi); Tony Vidrine, biologist manager, Louisiana Department of Wildlife and Fisheries, Opelousas; Mike Walker, biologist manager, Louisiana Department of Wildlife and Fisheries, New Iberia; David Walther, fish and wildlife biologist, US Fish and Wildlife Service, Lafayette; Dean Wilson, director, Atchafalaya basinkeeper, Bayou Sorrel, La.; Mark Wingate, composer, College of Music, Florida State University, Tallahassee.

Thanks also to the following helpful experts: Harry Blanchet, Marine Fisheries Division, Louisiana Department of Wildlife and Fisheries, Baton Rouge; Natha Booth, research microbiologist, US Department of Agriculture, Stoneville, Miss.; Antoinette DeBosier, resource scientist, forester, Louisiana Department of Natural Resources, Atchafalaya Basin Program, Baton Rouge; Denise Dooley, president, Ocean Pride Seafood Inc., Delcambre, La.; Sanford Hinderlie, composer and director, Music Technology Center, College of Music and Fine Arts, Loyola University, New Orleans; Sammy King, US Geological Survey, Louisiana Cooperative Fish and Wildlife Research Unit, LSU Ag Center, Baton Rouge; Carl Lindahl, research professor of English, University of Houston; Lise Olsen, investigative reporter, *Houston Chronicle;* Maida Owens, program director, Louisiana Division of the Arts Folklife Program, Baton Rouge; Paul Rudy, composer, University of Missouri, Kansas City; William G.

Stark Jr., museum division director, Louisiana State Museum–Baton Rouge; Kerry St. Pé, program director, Barataria-Terrebonne National Estuary Program, Thibodaux, La.; R. Glenn Thomas, director, Marine Extension, Louisiana Sea Grant College Program, Baton Rouge; Kim Walden, cultural director, Chitimacha Tribe of Louisiana.

Special thanks go to my research assistant, Kellie Smith, who helped me immeasurably in the final stages as proofreader and all-round sounding board. Her services and a number of my research trips to the Atchafalaya were funded by generous grants from the University of North Texas. Warm thanks as well to my dear Gulf Coast friends Ellis Anderson and Karen Ray, who several times in the course of this project opened their guest rooms to me, and to Emily Fox Gordon, George Sher, Ann and David Fairbanks in Houston, who offered me countless refreshing layovers during my travels. To the Thinking Like a Mountain Foundation, I offer deep gratitude for providing a perfect artist residency in the Davis Mountains exactly when I needed peace, quiet, and space to complete my work.

For constant inspiration and moral support, I thank my steadfast friend and collaborative artist Pat Alexander, who joined me on two extended trips in the Atchafalaya and produced a series of paintings based on her time there. For ongoing assistance and a lively point of view, I thank Charles Chamberlain, historian for the Louisiana State Museum. I am grateful as well to copyeditor Cynthia Lindlof for her interest, expertise, and precision. I offer heartfelt appreciation to Shannon Davies, my editor at Texas A&M University Press, whose enthusiasm for the project and sage advice guided this book to completion.

River Music

CHAPTER 1

Calls

E arl Robicheaux and I are driving east on I-10 in his little red pickup truck, slurping Community Coffee from to-go cups, chinning the irregular downbeats in *The Rite of Spring*. We don't know which Louisiana Public Radio station is broadcasting *Le Sacre* midday—Lafayette, which we've just left, or Baton Rouge, down the road—but we agree it's the perfect soundtrack for a bird-recording expedition in the Atchafalaya River Basin, the vast backyard Earl has prowled since childhood.

"I call it the Magical Kingdom," Earl says. "But it isn't Disney World—it's the real thing. Cage would have loved it—the whole basin is one big John Cage happening."

One can be reasonably sure my old friend is the only Cajun man on the road this morning talking about the pioneer composer of electronic and "chance" music—music in which at least one element is determined by a random process or performers improvising "in the moment." One can be equally confident Earl's is the only Louisiana pickup with both a fishing rod bouncing in the truck bed and a biography of the French Dada artist Marcel Duchamp (the one who turned a porcelain urinal into art) jammed in the glove compartment. Here, in two possessions, lies the paradox that is Earl: the outdoorsman who grew up around the swamp, gigging frogs from a pirogue, and the composer with the Ph.D. inspired by the most unruly imaginations in Western art. Yet his combined experience in Louisiana's wilderness and the hallowed halls of learning has made him an astute, poetic chronicler of the Atchafalaya environment: 1.4 million acres of earth, mud, and water stretching 140 miles, from the river's origin—peeling off from the Mississippi River at the ankle of Louisiana's boot—all the way to the Gulf of Mexico. The Atchafalaya Basin, encompassing "Cajun country," is North America's largest river swamp, and its troublesome fate is directly tied to longtime manipulation by government, industry, and individuals. In the past few years, Earl, now fifty-one, has devoted himself to documenting and expressing the basin's complicated story in sound, and as a fellow musician, I'm here partly to learn about how he does it, and more important, what drives him to do it.

· · ·

It's a gray day, but Stravinsky's jagged rhythms spark it up. We cross the West Atchafalaya Basin Protection Levee and enter I-10's longest bridge: an elevated concrete chute more than eighteen miles long, bisecting the Atchafalaya River and its multifarious waterways, marshes, and fugitive lands so ill-defined that distinguishing the river itself seems impossible. We continue over the great Henderson Swamp to a swath of dry land and take the Butte La Rose exit, looping down into the Atchafalaya Welcome Center's ample parking area. Like so many Southern welcome stations, this one is built to mimic an antebellum plantation home: long and white with green shutters, and a wide porch offering rocking chairs from which to view a freshly trimmed lawn and a hedge of Indian hawthorn in bloom.

Here, we're supposed to meet a ranger with the Army Corps of Engineers who will give us a key for a gate to an all-terrain-vehicle trail in the Indian Bayou Wildlife Management Area, a 28,500-acre tract north of the center. The trail, usually closed to automobiles, leads to an agricultural field and a beautiful swamp, Earl says, with a tree line perfect for sighting birds and recording them. Earl started his bird work in 2002, a few years after moving back to south Louisiana from Texas, where I met him. First he produced field recordings for Cornell's Lab of Ornithology but soon found uses for birdsong in original electronic pieces, as well as in wilderness soundscapes for educational exhibits, radio programs, and a CD that he hopes will help alert listeners to these vast, rich lands compromised by development.

Today he wishes to capture something new—what, it's impossible for him to say. Raised a French Catholic with altar boy credits, Earl is mostly a Buddhist, open to whatever happens to sing or growl or croak on a given day. And recently, he's been critically ill with cancer. This is his first outing since his chemotherapy regimen ended, and he's simply glad to be back in the swamp.

But we're more than an hour late for the ranger, because it's been a slow morning. Earl's elderly mother, Eula Thibodeaux Robicheaux, with whom he lives in Berwick, at the basin's southern terminus, has a cold, and first we had to run to the pharmacy for cough medicine and then to Cannata's, the local family market, for soup. Then Earl, easily fatigued, needed a rest and a shot of sugar from Ginger's Bakery down by the river. At Ginger's, the morning rush of shrimpers, oil workers, and police officers had subsided, and Earl took his time deciding between a bear claw the size of a catcher's mitt and a croissant bulging with chocolate.

He finally chose the croissant, accepting the wax-papered treat from the counter help, an upbeat, pony-tailed girl who called him by name. "I need to gain some weight, anyway," Earl said, taking the croissant in three bites.

"True enough," I said, glancing at his diminished form, swimming in a wrinkled khaki shirt and trail pants. Not long ago, Earl tended a respectable belly built on shrimp, crabs, and doughnuts.

"This is the only positive thing about going through so much chemo," he said. "Now that it's all over, I get to eat whatever I want."

. . .

Well, the ranger will be here, or he won't. Neither he nor Earl carries a cell phone.

Earl parks, straightens his cap, and presses a tan hand to his door latch, releasing it after three tries.

"You OK?" I ask.

"Yeah," he says. "But I could use more coffee."

We lope to the Welcome Center, me checking my usual brisk stride.

"Hear that?" Earl says, stopping, and I listen. Blackbirds. Carolina wrens. Cheeping, peeping, chirruping from beneath the faux-plantation home's eaves.

Like the house, the sounds are not "real"—they come from the eight nature sound recordings Earl was commissioned by the Louisiana Department of Natural Resources (LDNR) to create for the center, outdoors and in. Some sound fields were captured at Indian Bayou, where we're going, as well as adjacent lands in the Sherburne Wildlife Management Area, the Atchafalaya National Wildlife Refuge, and another Army Corps parcel that interlocks with the previous two. Those three total forty-four thousand protected acres—a fraction of the basin, which is mostly privately owned—and are managed as one unit by the Louisiana Department of Wildlife and Fisheries. Earl has also recorded east of here at Lake Martin, one of the largest nesting areas of wading birds in the country, and a top national bird-watching spot. But this year many birds have abandoned their nests, according to a ranger at Lake Fausse Point State Park, where I've been staying in the basin, reading, hiking, watching, thinking, renewing my love for swamplands.

"I bet the Lake Martin birds all moved to an area not so accessible to people," the park ranger, a retired biology teacher from New Iberia, speculated one afternoon. "Someplace with no guides and no airboats." I thanked him, and took to a quiet loop trail. Only a few steps past the trailhead, I met a red-shouldered hawk, resting on a branch, eye level to me. It did not move. I passed by, softly, my boot soles just pressing into the moist earth.

Although I am an outsider, or, as a Cajun might call me, "Le American," I confess I've not come here simply to document Earl but also to follow some inner compulsion, perhaps stretching back to my south Florida childhood, when my mother, a professional Girl Scout, hauled me alongside her into the Everglades, searching for unspoiled land the Scouts might lease for primitive campsites. Later, when I was a young woman following, by chance, a musical career to New Orleans, I often struck out on road trips to the Atchafalaya for no conscious reason. I only knew that the swamp drew me out of the city, and drew the city out of me, and I needed that. And although I didn't last long in New Orleans—in fewer than four years I decamped to Texas—I continued to return to south Louisiana, as if it were home.

Inside the plantation house, Earl and I pass tall ranks of glossy brochures and find the complimentary coffee bar: Community's tall red canisters, sugar packets, and a shaker of powdered cream substitute. A ferocious alligator bellows from the adjacent nature exhibit, and two little boys react, one giggling, the other screaming back at the invisible reptile. Earl smiles, amused and satisfied by his work.

"I got that alligator at Lake Martin," he says. "I'd gone up there to record a dawn chorus—was there by 5 A.M., you know, before the planes started flying in and out of New Orleans. I had everything set up, was running the tape, and all of a sudden, I heard this subaudio thing that sounded like a lion's roar. The needles on the recorder were going crazy.

Well, it was the mating call of a male alligator, so loud I thought it had crawled up under my car. But that recording impressed the guy at DNR, and helped me get the contract for this Welcome Center."

We ask the friendly retirees behind the information desk if they've seen a park ranger, and they haven't. Earl's alligator roars again, and this time a grown woman yells, "Whoa!" We refill our coffee cups and head back to the truck.

Passing under the I-10 bridge, we take a high levee road north toward Indian Bayou, rocking and bumping along the levee's crest, scattering rocks and dirt. Earl reminds me that the Atchafalaya's levees go back to settlement days, when Native Americans such as the Choctaw, Houma, and Chitimacha lived here. (*Atchafalaya* comes from the Choctaw language: *hacha* for "river" and *falaia* for "long.") Early embankments took shape from naturally accumulated materials; after the mid-eighteenth century, when Earl's French Acadian ancestors, expelled from Nova Scotia, found their way to a "New Acadia," landowners began raising the natural levees for flood protection.

But then, Earl tells me, came a chain of events leading to the Atchafalaya's compromised state and its cultures' dissolution. "You need to know this, to understand where I, the birds, and everything else in the basin are coming from," he says, and he lays out the history, beginning in his great-grandfathers' era.

In 1831, a steamboat captain named Henry Shreve dredged a passage across Turnbull's Bend, a loop in the Mississippi, a little over three hundred miles from the mouth. At the loop, the Red and Atchafalaya rivers met the Mississippi—the Red flowing into the loop, the Atchafalaya flowing out. By shortening the Mississippi River channel at that spot, Shreve cut short the route to the sea. Operating on far less knowledge than we have today, he set conditions for silting in the upper half of the loop and created what is known as Old River, the lower half. Old River linked the three rivers, so the Red River now flowed directly into the Atchafalaya, and Old River flowed out of the Mississippi into the Atchafalaya.

One might imagine that the Atchafalaya would benefit from increased flow, but it did not at first. Gumming up the works was a forty-mile raft of limbs, trees, and refuse clogging the upper river. The raft had extended and swollen over decades, at some spots appearing to be solid ground, alive with plants and shrubs. "You could walk across it," Earl says. The raft would have to be removed to make the Atchafalaya navigable, restore the flow of water downriver, and allow the Atchafalaya to draw more water from the Mississippi, reducing flooding.

The job took more than twenty years—"Louisiana time," Earl calls it. Citizens along the river took the first crack at it, setting fire to the floating jungle in 1839. Then the state stepped in with steamers and snagboats and finally did away with the raft by 1861.

Freed, the Atchafalaya could accommodate more Mississippi River water—a good thing, it would seem, when the big river flooded. "But not necessarily," Earl notes, as we chug along the levee. As the Atchafalaya, drawing close to 30 percent of the total latitude flow of the Red and the Mississippi, broadened handsomely, the Mississippi, seeking the shortest route to the sea, threatened to change course for the sixth time in its more than five thousand–year history. There was a chance that, at flood stage, it might rush right through Old River and into the Atchafalaya's waiting arms. The Atchafalaya could become the new Mississippi, stranding commercially important communities, like Baton Rouge and New Orleans.

Earl tells me that the federal government stepped in with several Swampland Acts to aid water control and land reclamation in Louisiana, including improved levees. From Reconstruction until the great Mississippi flood of 1927, the Army Corps of Engineers, active in the basin since the Louisiana Purchase in 1803, worked north to south to construct a high levee along the widening Atchafalaya. But the 1927 flood, the most extensive river flood in U.S. history, wrecked the plan, and from that point on, the Corps worked furiously on ever more complicated projects to control water in south Louisiana, driven by the need to maintain the Mississippi as it was.

One of those projects is the pair of protection levees several miles east and west of the Atchafalaya River; they are the basin's official boundaries. These levees and others, like the one Earl and I are riding on, plus channels, cuts, and canals dredged for commercial traffic tied to logging, fishing, and oil and gas exploration, are examples of attempts to turn the messy, willful Atchafalaya into a sleek route predictable as a water slide (and always secondary to the Mississippi). But over the years, so much scooping and piling exacted a high toll on the land, wildlife, and people, such as Earl's family, who once depended on the Atchafalaya's bounty for sustenance. These acts also failed to keep the Mississippi from veering west toward the Atchafalaya.

"So the big solution came when I was born," Earl jokes. On August 4, 1954, two days before Earl first drew breath in a Morgan City hospital, Congress passed the Watershed Protection and Flood Prevention Act, giving the Army Corps the go-ahead for the Old River Control Project, the most dramatic effort yet at keeping the Mississippi on course. The project, spurred partly by serious flooding in May 1953, comprises several installations lodged in the loop where the Mississippi, Red, and Atchafalaya rivers nearly knot up and adheres to a mandate that 70 percent of the Mississippi's and Atchafalaya's total latitude flow goes to the Mississippi and 30 percent to the Atchafalaya. This move ramped up threats to the cypress swamps, fishing grounds, and bird habitats that originally attracted Earl's French forebears to the region. More cuts and canals, oil and gas pipeline installation, and increased tree cutting followed, even though old-growth cypress had been completely logged by the turn of the century, leaving some forests too weak to regenerate properly. Earl, a member of the last generation with intimate ties to the Atchafalaya Basin, witnessed it all.

"The bountiful Louisiana my ancestors knew disappeared," Earl says. "After they started using the Atchafalaya as a floodway for the Mississippi, the basin began silting in, and it was harder to live off what used to be an advantageous mix of land and water. At the same time, there were agricultural changes, commercial pressures, and population growth. Rice fields became sugarcane fields, and now the cane fields are being developed by architects. So little by little, my species has lost its home."

* * *

Behind Earl's seat, the Nagra tape recorder jostles loose, and I work to jimmy it back into place with an old towel.

"Can't have anything happen to my Nagra," Earl says, swallowing the last of his cold coffee.

The Nagra is a portable analog machine, totally obsolete in these digital days, but Earl won't use anything else.

"I know I seem obsessed with live analog sound," he explains, "because I am. I researched my whole setup—the Nagra recorder, the microphone, the studio—for about two years. I use the same setup the BBC [British Broadcasting Corporation] has used for a long time, for the exact same reason I'm really into the live concerts from the 1960s. You get ambient sound, live presence, color, the intensity that digital sound just can't capture. You know, Keith Jarrett refused to play anything digital for the same reason. Acoustic instruments are extensions of the body. The universe is expressed in the highest way through human beings. So the way I look at it, analog is spiritual. Digital reflects the mass-produced, the manufactured, devoid of soul, the alienated individual."

Eight years ago, Earl had no idea the soul of a Nagra lay in his future. Then, he was living in a Houston apartment, working as an engineering assistant by day, composing *Remote Sensing,* a multimedia installation about the decline in the world's atmospheric/oceanic environment, by night. The project, archived until recently at Nicholls State University in Thibodaux, includes large, mounted data collages, a text and audio installation, and a video supplied by NASA's Goddard Space Flight Center and NOAA (National Oceanic and Atmospheric Administration). Earl had moved to Houston in 1996 at age forty-two after finishing a Ph.D. in music composition at the University of Texas in Austin, and thought about basing a serious composing career there. But back in Berwick, Eula Robicheaux began imagining stalkers and other urban ghosts around the house and repeatedly called the local police, who finally called Earl, the only child. (His father died in 1981.) There was no money for a caregiver, and besides, in Cajun culture, family cares for family, and sons are especially responsible for mothers. Earl hadn't lived in the Berwick–Morgan City area for more than twenty years. He would never have refused his mother, but the move back still needles him, occasionally.

"If I'd stayed in Houston, I'd have never bought the Nagra," Earl says, and I know where this is going, because I've heard my friend's not-altogether-convincing riffs on this subject before.

"If I'd stayed in Houston, I might have gotten more performances, eventually," he adds.

I say nothing. He pauses, reconsidering.

"It's just not what I expected," he says, "though I'm not one to predict things. Anyway, I'm here. This is what I'm doing. And I've always liked the idea of saving things that might get lost."

                                    •   •   •

I met Earl Robicheaux in Austin in the early 1990s, when he was working on his doctorate at the University of Texas. A clarinetist specializing in contemporary music, I often attended concerts at the university and remember well Earl's dissertation recital in a small performance hall, spring 1994. Unlike most male graduate students, who showed up for their degree concerts in pressed suits and ties, Earl ambled in wearing a nubby brown sport jacket and no tie in sight. I recall problems with electronic connections, someone tripping on cable running between the sound engineer's desk and the stage, and Earl running back and forth, trying to fix things. Audience members—mostly students, faculty, and friends—laughed good-naturedly, and a couple of pals yelled, "Good going, Robicheaux!" and "Typical, dude!" This was, and still is, common in new music concerts, and Earl, a boyish fellow about five foot seven with hooded brown eyes and a wing of thick, dark hair pitched over his brow, took it all as an opportunity for physical comedy, muttering, at just the right times, "No way, man," or, "This would happen to me."

But once everything got plugged in right, and the lights dimmed, listeners understood one thing that makes Earl Robicheaux tick. They could hear it in his *Silent Forests,* a meditative piece for piano and live electronics, and *Light Chop on Protected Waters,* for flute, clarinet, violin, piano, and an enormously vibrant percussion battery: ten toms, two snares, a large bass drum, four cymbals, one tam-tam, five gongs, a triangle, wind chimes, marimba, two vibraphones, and celesta. These instruments, capable of delicacy and force, from a limpid whistle to a muscular splash, represented an almost frightening range—but nature's power and mystery call for it. Earl's pieces sounded like water and trees and wind, sometimes peaceful, sometimes furious, always moving, at once adhering to a cycle and responding to shocks from without. When the concert ended, the audience applauded long and loud. I congratulated Earl, delighted to make a friend from south Louisiana.

. . .

We've been bouncing along for a good twenty minutes, glimpsing the Atchafalaya River down the weedy slope to our right through a wild line of hardwoods. To the left, a lush, scruffy landscape comprising bottomland oak, ash, and hackberry bends and turns with the wind. The sun finally slides free of the whitening clouds. Earl suddenly swings left, away from the river and down the embankment to a yellowish concrete building with an old air-conditioning unit drooping from a window.

"Maybe the ranger is here," he says.

We pull up, get out, walk around. No sign of a ranger or anything official.

"I thought this might be the ranger station," Earl says, distracted. Chemo brain, he'd call it.

I wait, wondering if I should take the wheel. I realize I will continue to debate this on future outings, but that it doesn't matter.

Earl mops his brow with a bandana, puzzles out the scene.

Some minutes pass.

"This isn't the ranger station," he says, and climbs into the driver's seat.

"OK," I say, and we take to the levee road once more. We'll poke around, discover what else there is to see today.

Now Earl cuts over into Sherburne and guides the truck onto another dirt road increasingly beset by low-hanging trees and vines. Finally, the path dead-ends between a small pond and the tail of a creek or bayou. We struggle to open our doors, kicking with our boots, and once free, are enswathed by mosquitoes. For a few minutes, we tread carefully through the mud and marsh with the Nagra, listening. But our repellent isn't working. We're slapping our arms and faces louder than any bird could sing.

Back in the truck, Earl muses a moment, disappointed. "Aww. You ought to hear this place at sunrise. Frog choruses—bullfrogs—it's electric, man!"

He taps the accelerator, and we wobble off through the jungle to Big Alabama Bayou, at Sherburne's heart, where we recognize official birding trails and signs picturing common glories: scarlet tanager, great horned owl, double-crested cormorant, Canada goose. The dense plant life and teeming insects in this moist, tropical basin attract half America's migratory waterfowl and support about two hundred resident bird species, though a few recently made the endangered list.

"If you don't believe the amount of plant life," Earl says, "look at a pollen map of the United States on the Internet. Everything is OK until you get to south-central Louisiana, which is vivid red, year-round."

We post ourselves on a well-maintained bridge and lean on the wood railing, watching the sky, now clearest blue. A swallowtail kite swoops across the bayou, then another and another, the sharp white and black underparts clean as tuxedos.

"Good breeding ground for them, this canopy," Earl says, pointing toward the banks. We lean over the water, in comfortable silence. A few fluffy clouds rise over the trees. "I've always found it really cool, just watching clouds and listening to Bach organ music," he continues. "Bach is a very pure expression of the inexpressible, the infinite, but put into a form we can absorb. I'm interested in things that mark time, and that make you aware of your place in the earth. Bach's music and the movement of clouds are two of those things—very elemental."

Earl leaves the bridge, sets up the Nagra and microphones close to the bank, and waits.

. . .

I remembered an outing from several years before. I was driving from Austin to New Orleans to attend Jazz Fest and called Earl from the road. He invited me to stop by Morgan City, across the Atchafalaya from Berwick, for dinner, and we met at a community picnic area along Lake Palourde where, on a cracked concrete table, he unfurled a great twist of newspaper and poured out a mess of crawfish. To go with it, he'd brought a six-pack of beer and a roll of paper towels. We set to the crawfish, pulling the heads to suck the juice, splitting the bodies for the meat. The sun was just setting, and a light breeze blew over from the lake, drying the sweat on our forearms. We spoke very little, concentrating on the food. When we had done in the crawfish and beer, Earl swept the remains into an empty oil drum near the table. "Gotta show you something," he said, walking leisurely toward his car. I followed, took the passenger seat in the gray Honda sedan he was driving then, and rolled down the window. The sky was black now and spread with stars, and the moon, full and creamy, had risen over the lake.

Where we went next, I couldn't say. Earl drove north past Brownell Park, the wildlife sanctuary he managed at the time, then turned down an unmarked road, and another and another, each one narrower than the last, until we were so far from the lights of town we might have been driving under water. Every so often, Earl would say, "We're getting there," or "Not here, but a place that looks like it." To me, everything looked the same: the dark, shifting tunnel of cypress and bamboo, the wild, attendant grasses, the bladed trail down the middle that barely accommodated the little car. Finally, Earl crept to a stop, turned off the ignition, and motioned me to step out into the night.

"Listen," he said.

And I heard the grand racket: blasts of cicadas, chirps of crickets, high hums of tree frogs, the tantararas of a thousand birds. Now and then a bullfrog contributed a resonant *boing*, like the striking of a loose kettledrum, and a Klaxon call from a large, unseen waterbird pierced the din. When the surging violin section of insects retreated, I heard the muted owls: "Who cooks for you?" And beneath this, the swish and swash of water along the edge of the raised trail, hinting at muskrats and alligators out for a late-night swim and a snack.

Earl and I sat on the hood of the car a long time, noting the massive crescendos, the higgledy-piggledy counterpoint, the unexpected pauses that nevertheless seemed agreed upon by the entire rain-forest philharmonic, as if a maestro had commanded a hush. After a while, the sounds began to take on qualities of shape and color: whorl of thrumming white, blaze of roaring red, blob of gong purple, stripe of squeak green, billow of whisper blue.

You don't have to be a musician to love this, to find yourself transported and transformed. These myriad voices, tuned and perfected before any human dreamed of a piano or a cello, tell stories far older than campfire tales—stories older than words.

. . .

Dean Wilson, an outdoorsman and naturalist who moved from Spain to the Atchafalaya basin twenty-five years ago to train for an Amazon expedition and fell so deeply in love with the basin he couldn't leave it, is one of Earl's good friends. The two have worked together in various efforts to promote the basin's safekeeping. A few years ago, Dean became the Atchafalaya's basinkeeper, part of the national Waterkeeper Alliance, a grassroots organization that supports waterways and their communities. Recently, he's trained his eye on the cypress mulch industry and its penchant for clear-cutting; he even convinced Walmart executives to stop buying Louisiana mulch, putting a dent in the market and making the "Heroes Among Us" feature in *People* magazine. Dean says he depends on Earl as a spokesman for the Atchafalaya environment because his friend has watched it change since childhood, as industry, in tandem with natural phenomena, has worked its way up and down the basin.

"Earl grew up here and understands the whole picture," Dean says. "He recognizes what motivates different people, and he has a feeling for the birds and the swamp that is unique. When you find someone like Earl, it's like finding gold in the sand. I just hope that, like the basin, his health will improve, and he'll be with us for a long time."

·   ·   ·

It's midafternoon now, and the sky over the bridge is clear of birds, save a few common egrets and an occasional great blue heron. Earl packs up the Nagra, with no comment as to what he might have captured—he'll save that for later. It's time to push out of Sherburne and return to Berwick. We need to pick up dinner for Eula—maybe, I suggest, we can stop at the Yellow Bowl in Jeanerette, on Bayou Teche, for étouffée to carry with us. But Earl wants Japanese, and we wind up at Sakura in Lafayette. We choose a low-lit table, order sushi, and wait. My friend removes his cap, runs a hand over his smooth head. I ask about his latest work with Dean and the presentations he's made since those for the Louisiana Black Bear Festival and the Louisiana Wildlife Federation. I ask about his oral-history projects, too. Lately, he's begun interviewing elderly basin dwellers and members of vanishing populations, like the Chitimacha, employing his ear for distinctive voices. His clients include agencies like the Louisiana State Museum and LSU Seagrant.

"Right now I'm like the one-armed man with his hand tied behind him," Earl says. "I can't get out and do much, yet, but if I survive this regimen, and the maintenance chemo, I hope to do more. I think my best role right now is to provide the nature recordings, and occasionally give talks. I want everyone to understand that this environment is a beautiful place, and the best way to do that is to interpret it in a healthy way. I don't mean ecotourism, and boat landings, and plastic swamps. I want to promote the idea of listening to the swamp. I want to show people I'm not just fighting for the Atchafalaya for the hell of it—there's something here.

"It's like the Amazon," he adds. "If we lose it, or even the memory of it, we—all of us—are in serious trouble."

Earl stretches, reaches for his bowl of miso soup to sip, relaxes into a private, more philosophic voice. "You know, I've thought all along—long before the cancer came last year—that the idea of giving up any sort of goal or direction, even temporarily, allows one to experience a sense of being in time. The world of people is so obsessed with order; to experience nature, instead of the world that humans make, as the 'real' world, is very freeing. Growing up here in the Atchafalaya was for me a way of connecting with that."

CHAPTER 2

Roots

For Earl, growing up in the Atchafalaya was more than the daily
business of childhood. It encom-
passed resonances originating
more than 250 years ago and still thrumming today. When, on the outing in
Sherburne, I asked him for an example,
he responded simply, "I carry it all with
me." But a few months later, on a visit
to the basin's southwest side, he offered,
by way of explanation, to take me to the
Acadian Memorial in St. Martinville.
We went, but I drove, because Earl's
doctors had recently discovered some le-

sions at the front of his brain that sometimes interfered with directional sense and landmark recognition. Just a week before, driving home from a checkup at Chaberre Clinic in Houma, he had overshot his hometown exit twice, not recognizing the three bridges that connect Morgan City over the Atchafalaya River to Berwick.

Now we pulled up to the Acadian Memorial's white, two-story building on St. Martinville's rustic town square, just a few blocks from Bayou Teche, once the Mississippi's main course and an important transportation route during the Acadian migration. Inside the memorial's cool exhibit hall, Earl ambled to the Wall of Names, bronze plaques commemorating about three thousand Acadian refugees identified in early Louisiana records.

"Here they are," he said, pointing to the plaques. Running our fingers down the raised lists, we found his Acadian forebears: Anne Hebert Robichaud, a widow with four children, and Pierre Thibodaux, on Eula's side. (Surname spellings, even within the same family, would vary over the years.) Both arrived in Louisiana in 1785, when Spain offered exiled Acadians living in France a chance to settle there, enhancing Spanish Catholic presence in the region. Seven ships of Acadians departed from Nantes that year; Anne and her children set sail on the fourth ship, and Pierre and his family took the sixth.

French Louisianans know well how their peace-seeking ancestors were forced from the Canadian Maritimes by the British when the French and Indian War started in 1755, and in years to follow. "Every family can tell its story, going back that far," Earl told me, and I wondered how many other Americans could say that. Many Acadians, like the Robicheauxs and Thibodeauxs, tend family trees ranging from oft-copied documents originally handwritten or punched out on manual typewriters to large, continuously evolving websites resembling the twists and turns of the Atchafalaya Basin itself.

Earl's forebears settled east of the basin along Bayou Lafourche, at the time a wide Mississippi River outlet, later reduced to a narrow, silted waterway after a dam was installed at Donaldsonville, where the bayou meets the Mississippi. Anne Robichaud married Pierre Auguste LeBlanc at Ascension Church, presumably at Donaldsonville, and after his death twenty years later, lived south of Thibodaux on part of Acadia Plantation, once a traditional working plantation with a master and slaves, today a master-planned community "designed to revive the warmth of small-town America."

Anne's children came of age in Louisiana, and in the next three generations, the family tree departed but a twig or two from French lines—in the photocopied genealogy Earl pulled from his back pocket, I saw common Acadian surnames such as Prejean, Simoneaux, Crochet, Guidry, Landry, Comeaux, Breaux, and Boudreaux, with an occasional Spanish twist: Figueron, Romero. His grandfather Cyrus married Alida Mendoza, and the pair moved west from Bayou Lafourche to Charenton, west of Berwick along Bayou Teche, to work in the sugarcane fields. Adam, Earl's father, was the fourth of their nine children.

Earl's maternal grandfather, Jim, and his family lived near Morgan City on swampland he owned on both sides of Bayou Boeuf—land that would one day attract oil-fabrication companies, as it lined a direct route to the Gulf. Originally known as the Schwinn Estate, Earl's great-grandfather C. M. Thibodeaux had bought the property, amounting to several thousand acres, and added it to holdings representing the C. M. Thibodeaux Corporation. Earl's received impression of C. M., who died before Earl was born, is that of a wheeler-dealer. "A lot of evil went down at the big house at night," he said. But if Great-grandpa C. M. was a hustler, Grandpa Jim was a fainéant with no head for business, much to his descendants' despair.

As we wandered about the Acadian Memorial, its multimedia exhibits and research center eclipsed by a striking thirty-foot mural of weary, hopeful refugees encountering the Louisiana wilderness, Earl made a distinction between this place and other efforts at preserving the Cajun identity. "I like the memorial because it honors the past and tells a story," he said, but he was quick to question newly begotten symbols, like the Acadian flag, designed in 1965. To him, the flag seems an anxious emblem, a desperate attempt, like pinning a bright corsage to a faded housedress. It's no surprise that the new "Cajun pride" emerged during his childhood, when rural life gave way to modernization, endangering a very old culture.

To be sure, modernization in south Louisiana wasn't like it was in, say, Chicago. It included late-coming improvements such as telephone service to basin dwellers, the paving of backcountry roads, and even, in some quarters, electricity. Earl remembered visiting his grandpa Jim Thibodeaux and his great-aunts Virginia (aka "Boosie") and Ida in his late grandfather's Bayou Boeuf mansion, which, in the late 1950s, contained exactly one reluctantly installed light bulb. "Modernization" had come about when the old folks' children insisted they wire the place.

"At first my grandpa and his sisters said no, there's no need for it," Earl said. "Finally, they agreed to put one light bulb in the kitchen, and they stuck it in a tub on the floor for the chickens, so they would have a warm place to lay eggs in the winter. Those people didn't need lamps. When the sun went down, they went to bed."

The postwar era in Louisiana also saw commercialized Cajun food and entertainment—for many outside the state, their first glimpse of Acadiana. I well remember Friday nights in central Florida, in the early 1960s, when my flat-tongued parents and their friends, all originally from the Midwest or Northeast, gathered around a record player to hoot at the newest album by chef and raconteur Justin Wilson, one of the first popular Cajun tale-tellers, known for the ubiquitous catch phrases, "I gawr-on-tee!" or "How y'all are?" Wilson's accounts of hunting and fishing fiascos tickled my father, who grew up on an Indiana farm and told his own versions of such stories. My mother said the comedian's elastic French reminded her of Acadians she'd grown up with in northern Maine. During her childhood, French Americans in that region were—and long had been—subjected to racial and cultural prejudice, and I got a whiff of it the summer I turned ten and attended a Girl Scout camp near the Canadian border. There, I learned from my tent mate Dottie Michaud the colloquial expression "Jeeze-um," loving the freedom of that long *e*, not realizing the biblical and cultural connotations. Two weeks later in Bangor, my Victorian grandmother, holding tight to her British heritage, forbade it the instant it sailed out of my mouth.

Earl doesn't take offense at Justin Wilson or any of the Cajun comics who followed him. "I don't have an opinion about it," he said. "You can make a case for saying Justin Wilson bastardized the culture, but at the same time, the guy's a great cook, you know? If a culture can make fun of itself and not take the English language so seriously, it's pretty cool to me.

"I look at it this way: there's the United States, and then, there's Louisiana. When you enter Louisiana, you are no longer taken seriously. All the things most people in the rest of the country would be offended by? People in Louisiana don't even care. Which is what I like about it."

● ● ●

Earl can chart recent steps toward modern life in Louisiana beginning with his grandfather Cyrus Robicheaux, who managed a sugarcane-processing plant close to Charenton. Cyrus, an unschooled man, lived with his family in a house right smack in the cane field. Adam Robicheaux was born there in 1908, attended school sporadically, and dropped out after the fourth grade to help his father. But at nineteen, fed up with field work, he borrowed fifty dollars from an uncle to take the train to New Orleans and attend barber school, an ambitious act for that place and time. He moved to Berwick and became the town barber, a volunteer fireman, and a popular city councilman. He also married, had two children, and was divorced at middle age. After a time, he met and married Eula, ten years his junior, who had married and divorced briefly in her youth and earned her living as an office worker in Morgan City. A few years after Earl, their only child, was born, a developer building houses close to town named one of the new streets for Adam—a mark of Adam's position in the community. Adam bought a two-bedroom brick ranch house at one end of Robicheaux Street, on a corner lot. It had a two-car garage and an all-electric kitchen.

"My parents believed, as did most of their generation, that the newly found mass-produced implements of convenience were the future," Earl wrote in an unpublished essay. "And, the future was good. It was boundless—it was progressive. It was Perry Como and Andy Williams and Groucho Marx."

In contrast to his father, Earl earned a music degree from LSU and in his twenties lived as far away from south Louisiana as Washington, D.C. Yet his D.C. sojourn, the result of his 1980 marriage to a pianist, lasted only one year. He hated his corporate job as a data analyst for the Planning Research Corporation and quickly found solace in the city's museums, particularly the Hirschhorn and the East Wing of the National Gallery of Art, containing the abstract expressionists he was drawn to; they correlated to abstract modern music forms he admired. On weekends, he and his wife escaped to hike in the Shenandoah Valley, where for the first time Earl reveled in mossy forest floors and waterfalls. But one day he stumbled across the September 1979 *National Geographic* story about the Atchafalaya basin and "back-to-nature" swamp dwellers Gwen Carpenter Roland and Calvin Voisin, photographed by C. C. Lockwood. Earl's heart exploded with homesickness. Within weeks, he persuaded his wife to move to Morgan City, where he found employment as a compositor for a local printer. Two years after that, the couple moved to New Orleans, and Earl improvised an artist's career, working for several printers, playing piano in restaurants, and writing serious music under composer James Drew, with whom he had studied at LSU.

One of Earl's earliest public performances took place in Christ Church Cathedral, the first non–Roman Catholic church in Louisiana. The venue seemed to symbolize a move toward another sort of change, for around the same time, Earl met a Zen practitioner at a dojo devoted to meditation and commenced serious practice himself. In 1984, his marriage ended. He remained in New Orleans until he felt the need to uproot himself once more, and in 1989 moved to Texas for graduate school. Yet Earl grew homesick from time to time, and even in Austin, with its myriad markets and restaurants devoted to regional and international foods, he found it necessary to make runs back to his home state for "the basics."

"I remember when I moved in with some new roommates," he said. "I had some doves and some turtle meat and some crawfish tails, and I said, 'I hope you don't mind if I put these in the freezer.' They said, 'Earl, it's OK—just don't eat them while we're here.' And I thought to myself, 'They would rather eat macaroni and cheese than try something like blackbird jambalaya? How come? Just because they think it sounds funny?'"

Today, Earl, one of the few Robicheaux and Thibodeaux cousins to attend college, and the only one to run the gauntlet for a Ph.D., lives with his mother in the Robicheaux Street house, more than fifty years old and looking its age. In the living room, furnished with dark, upholstered furniture and a dusty glass chandelier hanging from the ceiling tiles, Eula, now in her early nineties, sits with her walker, watching game shows, television news, and on Sundays, Mass broadcast from Lafayette. When she doesn't need him, Earl works in his bedroom, containing his sound studio: computer, monitor, electronic keyboard, speakers, and other tools jammed together on folding tables. His floor is a chaos of books, CDs, and DVDs. The walls are hung with Audubon prints and posters from contemporary music festivals. Outside, the lawn, like others in the neighborhood, bears a neat, whitewashed concrete statue of the Blessed Virgin. "Mom won't let me take her down," Earl says. "She thinks the statue has saved us from hurricanes."

• • •

From St. Martinville, Earl and I went hunting for more signs of his past, following various winding, indirect roads, swerving in and out of small communities, watching the sun shift swiftly left to right. Bayou Teche winked briefly, here and there, mocking any attempt to use it as a landmark. I mentioned the irony of tracing a water route by car—the past and present unavoidably intertwined—and Earl bemoaned he's the first of his line not to own a boat. He'd like one, though. A few hours before, we had stopped at a boatyard and peered at his ideal through the fence. It's a local boat he calls a V-skiff: a V-front, double-hulled aluminum craft made for river running.

"The Atchafalaya is so swift because of channels dredged by the Army Corps," Earl explained. "You need a boat that is heavy, takes waves well, and is sturdy enough to weather logs that would damage fiberglass hulls. Plus, once you get into the delta, you have less than a foot of draft. It's the perfect channel boat. You can negotiate a foot of water and not kill yourself."

Crawfishermen prefer a V-skiff with a water well in the bow. "It's designed specially for getting through water hyacinth—an invasive species, you know. When you run into that problem, you pull the plug in the well and let it fill with water, so the bow goes down. After the boat lowers, you can cut through the hyacinths like an icebreaker."

We remarked on the necessity of adapting to change, sighing just a little, and soon came upon a fairly new housing development called Willowcrest. Earl remembered when it was a rice field and made no secret of his distaste for the homes there.

"Prime real estate now," he said. "Look at that house over there—a monstrosity, sort of imitation Greek. Never have Doric columns been so bastardized. And see how high those dormers are cut? The design is just unsound." He groaned. "Coon-asses building with bricks."

Then he noticed a sign for Country Club Estates—a designation so commonplace a Google search yields more than five million entries.

"There used to be a slave community on that land. Look at that new mansion over there—the owners saved one slave cabin as a look into the past and put an enormous fence around it, probably with a lot of wood preservative. And they put in a gaslight. And an American flag, right on the cabin. Truly, truly pathetic.

"When I was born, there were still shell roads out here. This was not, by any means, a community that had been in touch with the twentieth century. But like I said, things have changed."

. . .

I've known Earl since his youthful thirties, and despite his love and practice of contemporary art, he has always spoken about Louisiana like an old-timer. He is one of those people who, hyperaware of generational shifts, and born at a potent crossroads in time, seem destined to chronicle and interpret the difference between what is and what used to be.

On this outing, for example, we passed several acres dedicated to cane, and the sight of it brought to Earl memories of bird hunting with his father in that very field, when Earl was just six years old. Back then the field, owned by a friend of Adam's, teemed seasonally with ripe farm vegetables, and father and son were invited not only to hunt birds on the property but to pick all the vegetables they wanted, as long as they took them from the inner rows, not close to the road, where onlookers might take the same liberty.

"Sometimes we'd end a day with three hundred, four hundred birds, mainly blackbirds, rice birds [red-winged blackbirds], doves, and every once in a while, a teal," Earl said. "We'd load them all in the back of Dad's Super 88 Oldsmobile. Then we'd go pick vegetables until our clothes were full of mud, and I wished we'd had a wheelbarrow, because I had to carry it all back. We'd fill the trunk with turnips and cabbage and mustard greens."

At home, Earl and his parents set to work, cleaning heaps of birds. "We'd wash them, peel the feathers, twist off the head and wings and legs. We had an assembly line, and it took two or three hours. A lot of the birds got frozen for later, but we'd always reserve about twenty or thirty for a jambalaya. That's all we made—jambalaya. Just put some roasted birds with a little oil, a little onion, and then add rice, and water, and let the bird flavor the rice. I can still taste it. Kind of like dove, or wild duck, but not as gamey.

"When I was staying in the hospital for chemo, I had this dream about blackbird jambalaya. It was my sixth chemo—every time you get another, you go down that much more, so I was in pretty bad shape, and I'd caught pneumonia on top of that. Well, it seemed the worse I got, the more I talked about blackbird jambalaya. The nurses thought I was crazy. I guess I was getting back to my childhood."

. . .

As a boy, Earl enjoyed fishing around here, too. He missed it this day, he admitted, as we turned onto a gravel road leading to Lake Charenton. He wished he felt up to a morning on the water but settled for explaining how, from the time he was very young, he and his parents spent regular weekends on this lake, where his father's brothers had family camps. If they got themselves into a boat early—say, 4 A.M.—they could catch all the fish, crabs, and oysters a large, extended family required for a weekend.

"At one time this lake was so big you could hardly see across it," Earl said, as we passed over Grand Lake gauge and took another gravel road threading north between Lake Charenton on the left and the Atchafalaya Protection Levee on the right. "There were hundreds of camps."

The environment here has changed markedly in the past forty years, Earl told me. In the 1960s, when he was in his midteens, the Robicheaux uncles were suddenly obliged to abandon their lake camps. The Army Corps had announced its intent to drain the lake and use the materials at the center to build up the protection levee, and since the camp owners were squatters on federal property, they had no choice. They picked up and left. Yet once the Corps got going on the project, it decided to drain only part of the lake. A few families ventured back, but the lake was diminished and folks were uneasy about what might happen next.

Earl acknowledges a deep-seated mistrust of the Corps among many longtime residents, explaining that after the Atchafalaya was designated a floodway for the Mississippi, people realized the basin didn't really belong to them. "Little by little, they relegated their desires elsewhere," he said. "There was nothing they could do about it. The basin wasn't a Louisiana state thing any more." He motioned toward some old dock pilings standing in low water. "Those might have been Uncle Pete's."

■ ■ ■

With some imagination, one can picture this flat, open grass bank as a ridge crowded with hardwoods, camps, and houseboats, all ringing with the music of family bands and the shouts of returning fishermen tying up with a day's catch. Cast back many hundreds of years ago, and you'll see much earlier squatters: Chitimacha men and women who migrated to south-central Louisiana, attracted by the Mississippi Delta's natural abundance. For a long time the villagers lived in thatched roof dwellings tucked into the swamps or along rivers, but when French colonists arrived in the early 1700s, the Chitimachas' isolated lives changed. For a dozen years they fought the French in a war ignited by the killing of a missionary and fraught with various skirmishes. The Chitimacha, devastated by the long conflict, were resettled along the Mississippi but nearly died out from European diseases and alcohol. Eventually, a few remaining families sued the U.S. government for title to tribal land, and in 1917, the Chitimacha were officially recognized by the U.S. government. Today the total number of Chitimacha runs to about 950, with one-third living on a 260-acre reservation in Charenton. Their native language is long gone; the Chitimacha speak English or Cajun French. They support themselves with the Cypress Bayou Casino out on U.S. Highway 90. When Eula Robicheaux was in her seventies and eighties, she often drove up with friends for recreational gambling.

In 2005, as part of "Voices of the Atchafalaya," an oral-history project documenting individuals' connections to nature in the basin, Earl interviewed eighty-two-year-old Leroy Burgess, a former Chitimacha chief and head of the tribal council, about his early years living within the basin and in the Charenton area. Burgess told Earl that in the 1920s, when he was very young, he, his parents, and his four sisters and brothers stayed in the basin part-time, living off the land and water. He remembered how the family weathered the 1927 flood in Charenton, then moved to a basin house on Fish Island, accessed through a canal dredged by the Williams Lumber Company. There, they made their living fishing, trapping, and picking Spanish moss for sale as bedding material. "We'd pick it green, make a bed out of it, wet it down, dry it, and in about two weeks, sell it," Burgess said. "We got about three cents a pound for it."

One thing they did not harvest was crawfish. The bayous were loaded, but nobody ate them, except occasionally, as part of a stew. The crustaceans were more commonly used as fish bait. "No market for them at all." The first crawfish seller Burgess knew moved to the area from Illinois in the early 1930s. "He was living on Charenton Beach," Burgess said. "He had a cage trap and put in a big old gar, and split him open, and he got sacks full of crawfish." The restaurant claiming to have first put crawfish on the menu, in 1927, is Earl's favorite, the Yellow Bowl, just up from Charenton.

At day's end, the Burgess children played games on the litter bank or romped with their two dogs.

"They were good rabbit dogs—they could pick one up on the run. Same with squirrels—they could catch them jumping between trees, get 'em before they hit the ground."

Sometimes the children smoked squirrels from trees. "We'd chase 'em in a hole, shove some moss in there, light it, and they gotta come out. And we'd knock 'em in the head."

Indoors after dark, the family maneuvered by kerosene lamps. If they happened to run out of kerosene, they put gasoline in the lamp, with a helping of salt. "The salt would take the power out of the gasoline, make it burn more slowly," Burgess said. Everyone slept in a cloud of mosquito netting.

Although the basin contained a few fixed settlements like Bayou Chene, a well-documented community that disappeared in Earl's childhood, victim of the 1927 flood and later, sedimentation, Burgess recalled "living all alone out there." Most people in the basin, he said, lived on houseboats and changed locations from time to time. Some even picked up and changed houses. "You'd have a house here, and then you might go on until you found another house." The Burgesses were as nomadic as the next family. After a few years in their Fish Island headquarters, they bought a houseboat and moved to Grand Lake.

• • •

Earl's friend Jim Delahoussaye, a retired biologist for the Department
of Environmental Quality who lives in Butte La Rose, confirmed for me
one afternoon the character of the old houseboat communities. He knows
whereof he speaks, having spent six years in the 1970s fishing commercially out of Charenton and taking oral histories from the fishermen of
Myette Point who taught him the trade. He is devoting his retirement
to writing a book about them.

"The communities were organized in ten locations in the basin,"
Delahoussaye told me. "Now, they were dynamic communities. You
might have twenty houseboats in one bayou, and the next month it
might be twenty houseboats, but maybe with only twelve of the original
people—eight new ones would be there, and eight others would be gone.
They constantly moved around like that. A lot of the time there were
little family groups of houseboats. So if the Couvilliers lived in Little
Bayou Pigeon, and the head Couvillier decided to go to a canal, they
would all move."

I wondered how these fluid colonies managed to supply themselves
beyond the fish and wildlife they caught. That was easy, said Delahoussaye:
fish boats, plying the basin regularly to buy from the basin dwellers, doubled
as general stores, carrying "everything from rifles to headstones."

At least one other purveyor noted the fish boats' success. The Reverend Ira Marks, charged by the Louisiana Baptist Convention in 1939
with starting a "French Mission" out of Jeanerette, acquired a mission
passenger boat dubbed *Good Tidings* and a barge-based sanctuary, *The
Little Brown Church on the Water.* For nearly ten years he and his followers
fished for men and women: the Catholics and unbelievers of the swamp.
They helped build churches and schools, as well as a small hospital in
Bayou Sorrel. But in 1948 the Louisiana Baptists decided the results did
not justify the cost, and Reverend Marks was called to Utah.

• • •

Leroy Burgess told Earl how quiet the basin was in the 1920s and 1930s.
"There wasn't much boat traffic beyond a push skiff or pirogue," he said,

noting that small inboard engines called "putt-putts" appeared there in the 1930s, followed by outboard motors after World War II. Most basin dwellers hunted locally, around the house or houseboat. "I hunted day in and day out and never saw anybody." But then the population increased, and years later, when Burgess finally gave up hunting, "you couldn't walk twenty feet without running into people from Ville Platte and some of those places. It sounded like a little war back there, so many people hunting squirrels. But it's all posted now."

The Burgess children's pastoral life ended in 1934, when government educational programs finally reached them and they were required to attend school. Once more, the family left the basin proper for Charenton. Leroy Burgess was twelve when he entered the one-room schoolhouse erected on the reservation. But within a short time, Burgess's father, obliged to make the family's living by himself, moved back to the basin to work on cutting the right-of-way for the Atchafalaya Protection Levee. He died two years later, in 1936. Burgess, with about two years of education under his belt, left school to work on a trading boat.

Burgess described the basin back then as a series of large, conjoined water bodies: lakes emptying into other lakes emptying into other lakes. Grand Lake, which I thought to be a misnomer when I first found the blue vein on a 2004 map, matched its designation when Burgess was a young man. (A Civil War era map shows a huge aqua orb.) But the Old River Control Structure's completion in 1963 and the 1973 flood led to an increased sediment load that settled in lakes and ponds, or in Burgess's words, "it brought all that silt from upstate, and it hit dead water here splat like that and filled it all up, and now we got nothing but a bunch of chutes out there."

Jim Delahoussaye offered a broader view of changes in the basin communities. "The generations before Leroy Burgess's were born on land and lived on land," he said, "and for one reason or another, they moved from a land-based existence with their families to a floating existence. Then in 1950, with all the things that happened in the basin, they had to leave the water and go back to land." Which is what Burgess did.

Although the floating communities gave up the water, they did not give up their houses—they simply moved them up to the levee and squatted there until the 1973 flood forced them to drag their homes further, to the backside of the ridge. During that twenty-three-year period, the newly landed citizens were obliged to acquire new living skills.

"They weren't new to people; they were new to this group of people," Delahoussaye said. "For instance, none of them could drive. They had no concept of what automobiles were. So they all promptly got automobiles and wrecked them—they did! I'm serious! It took them awhile to learn that a car was not a boat."

Basin residents' occupations changed, too. As the basin continued to silt up, so did commercial fishing become a less viable living, and a society once dependent on physical and intuitive skills, not literacy, had to adjust. Levee children went to school, and some continued on to college. They worked on the oil rigs proliferating in the Gulf, or in businesses in town, and some moved away from the region. Rudy Malveaux, an African American friend of mine whose ancestors lived around Opelousas, tells me his clan migrated to Houston, coastal Virginia, and the San Francisco Bay area in the 1950s because the oil companies weren't hiring blacks. But that's not to say the basin proper was entirely empty of people. A few remained, in houseboats floating on oil drums courtesy of the petroleum industry. Gwen Roland and Calvin Voisin, the idealistic couple Earl read about when he lived in Washington, were among them, building their house on a steel barge.

Today, the swamp contains scattered weekend camps and a few loners' floating shacks. On a recent trip with Basinkeeper Dean Wilson out of Bayou Sorrel, not far from Gwen and Calvin's former stomping and paddling grounds, I was shown one. The shack had no plumbing or electricity, though a line of solar panels shone from the roof. The occupant and his boat were gone, presumably on a supply mission.

. . .

Compared to Leroy Burgess and his own father, Earl identifies himself as a city boy. On this day, as we turned away from the lake and headed back to Berwick, he admitted his most traumatic childhood experience occurred not during a hunting expedition in the swamp but when he was attacked by his uncle Pete's pet chimpanzee at Pete's camp. I asked for the whole story.

A dry cleaner by trade, Pete lived with his wife, Gal, behind their shop in Baldwin nearby and must have needed a diversion from the constant reek of perchloroethylene. So he acquired an untrained chimp, named him Zip, dressed him in diapers, and kept him tied to a tree in the camp's backyard. Soon, Zip learned to slip the rope.

"The monkey would chase you and take stuff from you," Earl said. "Uncle Pete would just say, 'Oh, Baby Zip, come to Papa,' and it would lie like a baby on his shoulder. But I always thought, one of these days, the monkey's going to mean business."

Older family members suspected the same and asked Pete to leave Zip at home, but he refused. Then one weekend, when dozens of Robicheauxs and their friends had come to the lake to fish and party, Zip finally broke free of his lackadaisical training.

"I was just a little kid—six or seven years old—and small for my age," Earl said. "And some relative, an older cousin or something, pulled me aside for a private talk. This man had a daughter about my age who was mentally retarded and she had a crush on me, and it was her birthday. And he said, 'It would mean a lot to her, if you would have just one dance with my daughter.' I said, 'Oh sure, I'll do it.'"

So Earl made his way to Pete's camp where everyone was gathered, making music or dancing to it. Adam wailed on the harmonica; others played violins, accordion, drums, trumpet—whatever was on hand. "And there was always a washtub." In addition to French songs like "Jolie Blond" and music from Lafayette, the family played hits by New Orleans greats like Louis Prima and Louis Armstrong.

"For everyone else that night, it was a fun time, but for me, it was like entering hell," Earl said.

"Here I am, standing at the front of the room, and the little girl is in the middle, and the band starts to play. And all the ladies in the room are going, oh, isn't that cute, and I'm feeling more and more like a victim. I go up to the girl and we're dancing, but after about a minute I say, I've had enough of this, and I run out the back door toward the boathouse. And without thinking, I ran under Zip's tree. Well, the monkey must have thought I was another monkey, and he jumped me. I was full of adrenaline, and I started fighting with him."

Earl and the chimp took their struggle all the way to the boat landing—they were about the same size, Earl recalls—and in a short time, Zip got "really ticked."

"So I started to punch the thing, and he tried to strangle me. And I said, OK, we're going overboard, and we did. The water was about up to our chests. By the time one of my uncles came out to look for me, the monkey was trying to push me underwater. If he hadn't jumped in the water and grabbed the monkey, I would have drowned."

"Am I supposed to read some Darwinian symbolism here?" I asked.

Earl laughed. "I guess I'm the kind of guy who just makes it—who kind of slips through the cracks at the last minute."

As we turned into Robicheaux Street, I told Earl I'd already figured that out.

CHAPTER 3

Wildlife

B efore Earl and his parents moved
to Robicheaux Street, they lived
behind Adam's barbershop on
the Atchafalaya's west bank in
Berwick. The shop, on Front Street, was
one block from the river, near the railroad bridge, so close you could hear the
dusky foghorns and smell the fishy water,
the pungent catch on the docks. One
afternoon Earl and I took a walk along
dilapidated Front, whose once-thriving
businesses had collapsed years ago after
shopping centers claimed U.S. 90. Earl

remembered learning to fish with his father close to a crab-processing plant on the river, at a dumping spot for refuse. "It was catfish heaven," he said. "In thirty minutes, we could catch about fifteen fish."

Marvin Hardee, a shrimp wholesaler Earl interviewed for an oral-history project, made catfish traps of two-by-fours, chicken wire, and screen, filling them with crab hulls and catfish heads scrounged from Casso's, the catfish wholesaler next door. Several times a day Hardee winched up the traps, shoveled piles of catfish into buckets, and, completing the cycle of life and profit, sold them to the catfish wholesaler. "That's how plentiful things were in the river," Earl said.

To harvest shrimp, which are filter feeders, Earl and his father employed an old Indian technique Leroy Burgess also used in the basin: cut a willow or wax myrtle branch and sink it in the river for half a day. "When you pull it out," Earl said, "It's full of shrimp, and you shake it in a tub. You got seven or eight pounds of shrimp that way, back then. The river doesn't have those delicate life-forms any more, though; there's the boat traffic and so much diesel in the water. Plus the flood of seventy-three drove a lot of shrimp away."

When Earl was around eight years old, he went to work for his father, shining shoes in the barbershop. His rates depended on "how bad it was."

"If a guy came in with Gulf oil on his boots, it could be really hard to get it off. But I had a friend who shined shoes there a long time, and he taught me all his secrets when he left." The formula for Gulf oil, he said, contained alcohol. "And then, a lot of saddle soap."

The town's gentry dropped in regularly for shaves and haircuts and to discuss politics and LSU football with Adam, who, according to Earl, "knew everything that was going on." But once in a while, the usual drone was broken by a citizen running in to exclaim, "You oughta see what they caught at Casso's!" and Earl would drop his shoe brush and race down to the dock. Often, the catch was an outsize catfish, or a huge bloody turtle, freshly decapitated, lying on a drain on Casso's cement floor.

Earl knew how the beheading was done: when the turtle poked its head out of its shell, one man would jam the end of a broom handle down the throat to steady it, and another would chop it off with an axe.

"We're talking loggerheads that weighed two hundred, three hundred pounds," Earl said. "Little monsters. Big as a car. They sold the leg and tail meat for different dishes."

You didn't just grab a turtle like that and fling it into a boat.

"They would set up a trotline of chain underneath the bridge, with big alligator hooks at intervals. They'd put things like a dead coon or cat on them, sink the stuff, and run the line with a crew boat that had a winch on the back."

Living along Berwick's main business street, Earl also observed the town characters. There were the evangelical preacher and his wife who set up a podium across the street from the bar and pronounced everyone in the vicinity to be possessed of the devil. There was Sheik Nini, the police chief who routinely stopped by Adam's shop for the full deal: a shave, a haircut, and a shoeshine. Another police chief customer who went simply by "Cherry" was, Earl said, "your old Southern police chief." If word came of a scuffle, "Cherry would just sit back in my dad's chair and say 'hey, let 'em fight it out.'"

Louis Mahfouz ran the clothing store, employing a man called Pop who at first terrified Earl. "He was hunchbacked and kind of snaggle-toothed, which would frighten a little kid, but he turned out to be nice. And you know, Pop is still alive—I saw him working at Walmart."

•   •   •

Earl would agree that his grandpa Jim Thibodeaux over on Bayou Boeuf would have counted as a town character—that is, if Jim Thibodeaux had ever come to town. According to Earl, Jim; his Irish wife, Novey Rogers; and their seven children, including Eula, originally lived in a house Jim built on the bayou's west bank, across from the "big house" C. M. Thibodeaux occupied. Jim didn't work; his father's holdings enabled him to live as a bayou gentleman. A short man—about five foot two, Earl says—Jim favored a small, brimmed hat and a pipe. But size didn't keep him from straying—what else was a bayou gentleman to do in his spare time? Eventually, Earl's grandmother found out about her husband's girlfriend and divorced him. Jim moved to the original family home directly across the bayou, where his aunts Boosie and Ida had lived together following C. M.'s death. They were only too glad to fuss over their nephew, who they insisted, even when the Depression hit, was "too small to work."

Although Jim paddled back across the bayou often enough to visit his children, his former wife, sons, and daughters were eventually forced to leave the scene to earn their livings. Six children scattered to New Orleans and East Texas to find jobs; Eula quit school in the eleventh grade to go to work in Morgan City, alongside her mother. "It was awful," she told me, one afternoon on Robicheaux Street. "Everything was cheap. Like beans and rice and all were fifteen cents a pack, or ten cents, and some things a nickel. But we didn't have the money to buy it." Eula and Novey found their first jobs at a seafood company, picking crabs. "We made seventy-five cents the first day," Eula remembered. "And Momma and I looked at each other, and I said, 'Do you think we can make it?' 'Oh, yeah, we'll make it,' Momma said."

From there, Eula clerked in a Morgan City department store, followed by a job as a desk clerk at a hotel. Then came a dry goods store, a grocery store, and the *Morgan City Review,* the local newspaper, where she ran the addressograph for about eight years. "When the war started, I sent papers to the boys overseas. Nobody ever missed a paper," she said, proudly. Until her last job, Eula walked about two miles each way, to and from work, and sometimes walked home and back for lunch. "I did a lot of walking—maybe that's why my heart's not too bad." She finished her career in a bindery run by King-Hannaford. In 1952 she married Adam. She stopped working two years later, when Earl was born.

* * *

Until he reached his teens, Earl visited his grandpa Thibodeaux and the great-aunts on Bayou Boeuf one or two weekends a month during summer, and occasionally on Saturdays, with his mother, in the winter. The old house, once a stately, columned mansion with a bushy swath of iron plants running from the dock to the veranda, had by that time been cut in half.

On a previous afternoon, Earl and I had driven over to the opposite bank—as close as we could get, given the oil-rig construction going on there—and glimpsed the derelict house through some trees.

"At some point the old folks said, 'Look, the house is too big; we don't use but half,'" Earl explained. "It was weird to me, as a kid, because there were doors inside that led to nowhere. I don't know what they did with the other half of the house—if they burned it, or used it for firewood, or what."

In the company of three French elders—great-aunts Boosie and Ida, and his grandpa Jim—Earl learned what he calls "the fine art of hanging out." Sometimes he roamed the shaded grounds alone, or picked pecans with his grandfather, or helped his great-aunts run a trotline for catfish. "We just caught enough for the day, because they didn't have a refrigerator," he said, reminding me that chickens had been granted the only electric service on the premises. Other than that, there was a good bit of porch sitting and mosquito swatting by the slow-moving bayou. "And in the winter, there were a lot of days when we would just sit in front of the fireplace, and the only sounds were the wind, and Aunt Ida, grinding coffee."

"There was something weird about Aunt Ida," Earl said.

"She always dressed in black—ever since her husband died, which was many years before. I remember some nights when I couldn't sleep. They'd put me in one of those big bedrooms, with a four-poster and mosquito netting, and I would lie there, wide-awake. I was used to a fifties house, you know—this was such a different world."

And then, suddenly, Earl would hear footsteps in the hall, "and the shadow of a person, and oh man, it was Aunt Ida carrying a kerosene lamp. And she would come to my bed, and bend down, and whisper, 'Sleep—sleep—sleep.' Sometimes she would get me up, take me down to the kitchen, make me some warm milk, and tell me a little bedtime story. She'd always say, 'There's nothing to be afraid of here.' But she looked like a witch."

Aunt Ida in perpetual widowhood was as mythical as the neighbor known as "The Philosopher." Remembered by some as Alcide, but identified by others as Thais, The Philosopher was a hermit who lived in a little shack along Bayou Boeuf, catching fish for his dinner and growing his hair to his knees. The story goes that Alcide proposed marriage to a girl who jilted him, and, grief-stricken, he went away to college and returned to the bayou to think—for the rest of his life. Any scholar would nail the tale as classic folklore, but Eula remembered the man: "Alcide with the long hair? Well, he died." Earl says Alcide likely descended from one of his great-grandfather's eleven children, and Earl's cousin Rose, ten years his senior, told me several members of the Felix Thibodeaux branch lived along the bayou. "They had long beards and dressed like in the 1800s," she said. Earl cited Robert J. Flaherty's 1948 film masterpiece *Louisiana Story*, about a twelve-year-old basin boy entranced by an oil rig in the swamp. As the boy makes friends with the oilmen, a silent old-timer watches everything from behind the trees. "Some of the Thibodeauxs were like that," he said, and I noted our similar position sixty years later, two artist types in old jeans and T-shirts, peering at the halved house and the rigs.

For some time after Eula and Adam married, Earl said, Adam planned to rehabilitate old Jim Thibodeaux, but nothing came of it.

"In the world of my dad, everything was clean. He's a barber, he's a city councilman, and Grandpa's like the old guy in the woods. Dad had an idea that he would give Grandpa a haircut, shave him, and buy him new clothes. But Grandpa didn't want that. He rejected it all. That's just the way he was."

⚬ ⚬ ⚬

Adam may have been an up-and-comer in town, but his family ate plenty of wild game captured in the swamps. As Earl and I turned from Front Street and strolled out to the river, he described group family suppers in the 1950s and 1960s, when his parents and two or three other couples would get together to cook and eat what the men had caught or shot or trapped.

"We didn't eat like we do today, out of the grocery store," he said. "There was always rabbit stew, rabbit sauce piquant, squirrel sauce piquant, rabbit spaghetti, chicken spaghetti, red fish court bouillon, catfish court bouillon, things like that. We ate wild game at least once a week."

Often, Earl and Adam hunted ducks and rabbits on Belle Isle, an island in Atchafalaya Bay, staying in a borrowed houseboat by the camp of a nutria trapper known as "Old Man Bijou." Old Man Bijou could score several hundred nutria in one day, according to Earl. At the time, the semiaquatic rodents, resembling a cross between a rat and a guinea pig, but a lot bigger, were valued for their fur, selling for two or three dollars a hide. Several times a year, a relative or middleman pulled up in a shrimp boat and Old Man Bijou loaded it with thousands of pelts—as many as sixty thousand at a time, Earl estimates.

"He was probably rich, but he and his wife didn't seem to need anything. They left all their money to their kids. They actually ate nutria—they baked it. It wasn't that bad, though at that time I'd eat anything."

One day, Earl and his father got curious about another nutria trapper named Pierre Lodrigue and took their skiff through an elaborate system of overhung bayous to find him. Motoring in to Pierre's camp, they sighted his grandchildren skinning hides together on the bank. Pierre was out trapping, and his wife invited Earl and Adam indoors for a bowl of stew. In time, a grandchild announced Pierre's return, and everyone scurried out to the wharf.

"First we saw a bateau so low in the water it was close to sinking. There was a high mound of nutria; he was completely loaded down. Finally we got to see Pierre. He was about five feet tall, with a cap and a pipe. And as soon as he pulled up, all the grandkids started unloading the things and skinning them."

● ■ ●

The nutria story in the Louisiana lowlands began with high fashion. In the 1930s, the South American herbivores were brought to the state for fur farming, in response to demand from Europe's tastemakers. Though the U.S. Bureau of Biological Survey cautioned the Louisiana Department of Conservation's Fur and Wildlife Division against introducing a new species, fur farming commenced, and in a short time, some of the razor-toothed animals gnawed their way out of their pens. What made this an environmental catastrophe was the nutria's spectacular reproduction rate. Sexually mature at about eight months, they mate year-round, and females may enter estrus but a day after birthing a litter, as many as twelve pups. In his 2002 article "Reconsidering the Origin of Nutria," published in *Louisiana History,* historian Shane K. Bernard wrote that one of the earliest nutria farmers, E. A. McIlhenny of Tabasco sauce fame, found that in fewer than two years, his original twenty on Avery Island had multiplied to "probably 500 to 1,000 animals." The stage was set for profit, and environmental peril.

By the time Earl was a child, a nutria glut had caused prices to fall and trappers to leave the business, as the pests gobbled crops and marsh vegetation. To help the trappers and protect the wetlands, the Louisiana Department of Wildlife and Fisheries stepped in to find new markets for the creatures, and during the period when Earl and Adam camped next to Old Man Bijou, Germany imported more than a million nutria pelts a year. In 1981, the going rate averaged eight dollars a pelt. Then the market tanked again. To blame were the decreasing fashion popularity of fur (wrought partly by animal rights concerns), the 1987 stock market crash, and fur overproduction in Europe. Today, nutria damage is a major concern. The voracious animals have devastated thousands of acres of marsh, though the Coastwide Nutria Control Program, begun in 2002, has managed to slow the process that simply goes, vegetation is eaten, soil erodes with the tides, elevation drops, and *voila!* Open water.

While based at Belle Isle, Earl and Adam went after ducks at a place called Fish Trap Canal, "teeming with mallards, pintails, all kinds of canvasbacks. I didn't know what I was killing." Another area they liked was East Cote Blanche Bay, west of Belle Isle and peppered with small islands hopping with rabbits (and crawling with nutria). Formed by sediment from the Wax Lake Delta, which emerged after Wax Lake was dredged in 1941 to make a flood relief canal off the Atchafalaya River, these islands attracted many animals that nested in mashed river cane and dug miles of trails and tunnels. Often, father and son would motor out with a few of Adam's friends, each taking an island alone. In the winter, temperatures there often dropped below freezing, "so if you killed a few rabbits and put them in the back of your hunting jacket it helped warm you up."

Earl described a typical day. "They'd drop me off on an island and say, 'Here's a dog. We're coming back in a few hours.' So what happened was, the dog would chase a rabbit to where the perimeter of the island had a little levee, and the rabbit would hop in the trench for protection. Rather than wait down there for the rabbit, where he could see me, I got up on the levee and watched the chase. I could hear the dog, and the rabbit coming in front of him, and I'd pull the trigger of my little .410 so it made a click, and the rabbit would hear it and stop. That's when I got him. I shot a lot of rabbits that way."

Earl also cleaned a lot of them—the day's take. Tradition held that the youngest hunter did the honors.

"The way you do it is, you put a nail on a tree, then you find the little tender spot between the bones and the tendons of the rabbit's back legs, and you sort of pop the rabbit, head down, on the nail, right at that tender spot. Then you make a fine cut, just to get your hand in the fur. And you pull down, basically peel the fur off the skin till you get to the head. You pull all the guts out, and normally you cut the head off. But oh no, not with my dad around! He always wanted to eat the rabbit brains.

"So once I told him, 'OK, I'm the one out here cleaning the rabbits, and we've got twenty-five or thirty of them. I'm not taking home all those heads. I'm telling you right now, you get two heads: two and only two. It grosses out Mom, it grosses me out, and if you want any more, come out and do it yourself.'"

But such bounty, Earl learned, could disappear almost overnight. On one outing, he asked to be dropped on a rabbit-rich island he'd hunted the year before and was surprised to find it desolate. Gone was the vegetation that had sustained four-footed life. The animals, having reproduced beyond the limits of their habitat, had died or moved on. Earl saw it a lesson in delicate balance—one that could apply to any species, including humans.

▪ ▫ ▪

I thought about Earl's story one morning when I paid a visit to Tony Vidrine, Region 6 manager for the Louisiana Department of Wildlife and Fisheries in Opelousas, in the northern half of the Atchafalaya Basin. This was another of the several conversations with experts I sought, to fill out the basin's profile.

Tony invited me to sit on a couch across from his desk, and to make room for my gear, I had to shove to one side a huge clear plastic bag of fur.

"What's this?" I said. "Been hunting?"

"No," Tony said, "those are rabbit pelts we use for school educational programs. We pass them out to the kids, to handle. So many these days haven't even seen a rabbit."

When I expressed surprise, Tony continued.

"You know, you hear people all the time talking about doing anything to get their kids out of the house away from that video game. They get addicted to that stuff. So we try to provide ways to get kids involved in bird-watching, hunting, and fishing so maybe they'll see it, stick with it, and like it. To make a good-quality youth hunt, we put kids in areas where they'll have an opportunity to see deer and ducks and turkeys and have a better opportunity to take one. And the hunts work well. We've had a lot of applicants. And a lot of kids who come through there tell us they've never been hunting, that it's their first time they've taken an animal." He paused. "You know—anything to get the kids outside."

Tony pointed out that hunting with dogs, as Earl and Adam and several generations before them did, has all but died out. Some hunters today don't want to deal with the physical upkeep; others feel dogs are a disturbance in the wild. There's also the expense. Earl's uncle Wilbur, who Earl admits was "really out," bred and trained beagles for hunting and was so afraid of dognappers that he wrapped his kennels with electrified barbed wire and erected "little alarm stations with light towers on them that literally swept the area all night long."

But the main deterrent has to do with landownership. In the 1960s, when the Robicheaux men hunted, they—and their dogs—went just about anywhere they wanted on open land, public or private. In the 1970s, private landowners and timber companies, smelling potential profit, started posting their land and selling hunting leases. The use of dogs plummeted—what dog can read a boundary marker?—and hunting clubs formed, with outdoorsmen pooling resources to purchase an annual lease for the group.

Most landowners lease year to year, though some have gone to five-year leases, Tony said. And prices have gone up. Ten years ago, basin land leased for hunting at two to three dollars an acre. In 2009, the average price was eight to ten dollars an acre.

As a result, the number of hunting clubs and members in them has skyrocketed. Their top target is deer, followed by waterfowl, small game, and turkeys. Tony says there are hundreds of clubs leasing land in the basin.

"When I first started working here twenty-six years ago, we used to keep track of how many club members there were per acre. One member per one hundred acres was average. Well, now it's probably one member per less than fifty acres. They've had to increase club membership to pay off the lease, because instead of paying five thousand dollars for a lease, they're now having to pay ten thousand dollars."

In fact, after oil and gas, hunting is the most profitable enterprise in Atchafalaya Basin—not surprising, given that most of it, roughly 1,327,500 acres, is privately owned, compared to the 72,500 acres overseen by the Louisiana Department of Wildlife and Fisheries. So, while offering a kid a small rifle in exchange for a PlayStation console may introduce him or her to the glories of nature and the satisfactions of outdoor sport, it also helps develop a new generation of customers for hunting leases. The basin should be able to accommodate those seeking four-footed prey, since, as the region silts in, the amount of land will increase. It's worth mentioning here that in Louisiana, land accumulated by siltation belongs to the landowner on whose property the new acreage has attached itself.

· · ·

Earl has confessed that he and Adam sometimes hunted for squirrels illegally, from a boat, around Lake Verret, because otherwise, "they can hear you coming for miles." He didn't like tracking them in the woods; it was too dangerous. The last time he tried it, he was twelve, out hunting with a group of his father's friends.

"There's always the possibility of stepping on a snake. Rattlesnakes love to get on ridges, and you need to get up on one in order to see the squirrels. Since you can't always be looking down, you might find yourself surrounded by them, or by swamp spiders. That day I walked into a whole den of copperheads. A lot of little babies and stuff. I had an idea they were poisonous, so I instinctively backed out, real slow."

Earl returned to his dad's pals, who were sitting around drinking beer, and told them about the copperheads. "And this guy said, 'You mean to tell me you went in there without a .357? Man, they got a lot of wild boar out there. And if they find you, and you're between a female and her young, they're gonna come after you.' And I said 'That's it, I'm finished. No more squirrel hunting for me.'

"I've always been very conscious of what guns can do," Earl said, "and a .357 for a twelve-year-old kid? That's a big gun. A fairly substantial bullet. That'll blow a man's brains out. Completely destroy his skull."

• • •

Although he stopped hunting, Earl never lost interest in fishing. He and Adam shared that passion for years, plying the waters in a bateau or their fifteen-foot fiberglass tri-hull, depending on where they wanted to go. They fished both inside and outside the basin, in lakes and bayous near Morgan City and in Atchafalaya Bay.

"I remember all the freshwater clam lakes between Morgan City and Houma," he said. "Sometimes we got out on several ridges close to the coast and looked in the woods, and found big clam shells. That's the way the barrier islands were built up, with these shells, and they were the first to go, dredged to build roads. They were the first line of defense against wave action."

The pair harvested lake oysters by hacking chunks from a reef with something heavy, like a sledgehammer or posthole digger, dumping the chunks in the boat and taking them back to land to hammer apart.

Often, father and son went crabbing. The night before, they spent two or three hours making long lines hung with bull lips, bought packed in salt, and very tough. They'd stuff the baited lines in a bucket and in the morning go out to a bayou near the bay. There, they strung the line out across the water, then turned the boat around and just paddled along, pulling the line, dipping up the crabs hanging onto the detached lips, kisses of death.

Other times they might simply toss some fish heads in a dip net or hoop net, sink it, then yank it out right away. "You'd have two or three crabs there—they love blood."

Still, bull lips were best. "They really hold up," Earl says. "Sometimes as long as a week."

As with hunting, fishing in and around the basin has become less motivated by basic sustenance or the requirements of a particular home-made dish, and more by commercial interests and recreational sport. Sometimes commercial and weekend fishermen don't see eye to eye. Earl remembered when New Orleans chef Paul Prudhomme started the craze for blackened redfish, or red drum, in 1979. The fish, which prefers salt water but also tolerates well the saline–fresh water overlap in the coastal marshes, like those in the Atchafalaya Delta, seemed less plentiful to Earl, who was still casting in and around there. "When K-Paul's started blackening it, we saw the stock diminish," he said.

"The 'redfish craze' sparked research into the age structure of the adult red drum in offshore populations," explained Louisiana Department of Wildlife and Fisheries finfish expert Harry Blanchet, when I inquired for details. "That research indicated that harvest rates on the inshore fishery were too high in the 1970s, and this was being reflected in the purse seine fishery during the 'craze.' As a result, more stringent measures were put into place for recreational and commercial harvesters."

Those measures included size limits for both groups, lower creel limits for recreational fishermen, and a quota for the commercial side. Shortly thereafter, all commercial harvest of red drum was outlawed, and gill netting was banned. Little has changed. The size and bag limits for 2010 have been in place since the 1980s, Blanchet said.

For the sport fisherman, which Earl aspires to become again, the year-round limit on redfish is five. Blanchet said that under the current regulations, red drum are not overfished by conservation standards, and there are enough juvenile fish escaping to spawn and maintain the stock.

Fishermen complain, from time to time, about fluctuating regulations. But the state's rules are nothing like the frontier justice still alive in the swamp when Earl was a boy. As he and I left the riverfront, he told about a day in the 1950s when he and Adam went fishing with the pipe-puffing nutria trapper Pierre Lodrigue. Turning a bend in the bayou, Earl said, they spied two fellows running some of Pierre's trotlines.

"Pierre pulled out his .22 and popped the line at a hundred yards. 'You see what I just did?' he yelled. 'Just imagine if that was you! You know that's not your line—you probably don't even *have* a line.'"

The guilty men swore never to do it again. Pierre hollered back, brandishing his rifle, "No, you won't—never—not around here, buddy."

I asked if Pierre would really have shot the thieves for a second offense, and Earl didn't hesitate to answer.

"Sure. Are you kidding? That was Louisiana, man."

CHAPTER 4

Basin Education

I f frontier justice was alive in Earl's
lifetime, so was frontier education.
Though the school boat days were
long gone, Berwick High was sometimes short of teachers, and in 1969,
when Earl enrolled there, hoping for
instruction in biology, he signed up
for a course taught by Randy Dooley,
a faculty member hired on the fly with
no teaching certificate. Dooley, now a
retired physician living in Patterson,
about thirty miles from Berwick along
Bayou Teche, is the son of a Delcambre
shrimp processor. He was educated in a

private Catholic school in New Iberia and the University of Louisiana, Lafayette. Earl credits him with opening his eyes to the richness of the Atchafalaya environment. But Dooley never intended to teach, he told Earl and me one day, over coffee in the historic home he lives in and is renovating, room by room. He planned to become a research biologist and in 1969 began studying for a master's degree in biology at the University of Louisiana, Monroe.

Biology

Dooley explained he lasted one semester in Monroe—not because he couldn't do the work but because the Vietnam draft had just begun, and he drew a low number in the first round. He remembers the day the official letter arrived, ordering him to New Iberia for examinations. He drove down from Monroe, passed his exams with flying colors, and was ordered to Pope Air Force Base in North Carolina to train for service in Vietnam. Then, just as he was preparing to leave Louisiana, he received a second letter ordering him to another meeting in New Iberia. Puzzled, he appeared the same afternoon to meet with the officer in charge. "You're very lucky," the officer announced. "You have a choice. You can go to Vietnam for two years or teach school in St. Mary Parish for three."

The thought that three years teaching the children of Baldwin, Berwick, Franklin, Patterson, or Morgan City was deemed equivalent to spending two years in Vietnam never crossed Dooley's mind. He was just plain confused. The officer explained the deal: the St. Mary School system suffered a teacher shortage, and the New Iberia draft headquarters had agreed to funnel likely candidates its way. Dooley protested: "I'm no teacher; I'm just a biology student!" and the officer replied, "It doesn't matter—they need you. It's your choice." "I guess I'm going to St. Mary," Dooley said.

Dooley arrived at Berwick High in January 1969, to teach general science, biology, and study hall, and still remembers how awkward he felt.

"I had no friends, no one who wanted to show me how to teach," he said. "The principal had done a poor job with his staff, and there was a lot of animosity. He even listened in on classes through the intercom at the back of the room—he'd had the light removed from the speaker box so the teacher couldn't tell the thing was on. But there was a little pop when the principal tuned in, and the kids in the back could hear it, and they'd wave their hands. The kids and I, we just clicked, maybe because I wasn't much older than they were, and it got to where, if we knew the principal was listening in, we'd start laughing and screaming and hollering."

That put Dooley in a weak position as disciplinarian, at first, and one day he was forced to announce to an unruly biology class, "If you're going to act like vegetables, you'll have to sign your name like vegetables." He posted a sign on the classroom door labeled "Vegetable Patch" and for the rest of the term would only accept homework papers with signatures like Lettuce LeBlanc, Tomato Touchet, or Radish Robicheaux. "They were mad at me, and they stayed mad at me," Dooley said, "but it worked."

"So Earl got a person who couldn't teach," Dooley said, passing us a plate of croissants. "But the kids made me want to give them everything I knew—their eyes were so open—and I tried to teach them, like the teachers I loved the best had taught me."

Earl replied, "You deepened my knowledge of the outdoors here. I'd taken it for granted."

Dooley described Earl as "one of the nerdy ones" who chattered earnestly about quasi-philosophical matters and trundled after him outside class, asking questions. In class though, Earl was not always so talkative. "The mark of an only child," Earl observed, but Dooley said he recognized a young man striving to make sense of the world beyond a hot, south Louisiana schoolroom.

"Sometimes he would come in the room very quietly, and he would be there, but he would not be there," Dooley said. "Something was on his mind; you could tell when he was up and when he was down. But he was a good student."

Unencumbered by learning theories, Dooley grabbed natural teaching opportunities as they came. When he arrived at Berwick High, *The Undersea World of Jacques Cousteau* had just premiered on television, and the students were so excited about it, he built it into his biology course. Each week, he gave the class a ten-point quiz on the latest episode.

"Some said, 'It's not biology!' And I'd say, 'Sure it is; it's water biology.' So their families were forced to watch Jacques Cousteau, even though the father might want to watch the fights. Maybe everyone in the household learned something. Maybe."

Dooley's youthful, seat-of-the-pants approach to teaching attracted eighteen devotees who followed him to advanced biology. When he understood how ravenous they were for information and experience, he tossed out the textbook and, with the blessing of a new principal, planned six units based on his master's courses. All required hands-on work, far more adventurous than dissecting the usual mail-order frog.

For example, there was the snake-catching assignment: two per student, one poisonous, one nonpoisonous. Earl remembered some of the girls paid the boys to catch theirs, and the division of labor continued in the classroom. The boys seined for minnows in a ditch in back of the school, and the girls fed the minnows to the snakes. The idea was to increase the kids' comfort around snakes, to learn which were poisonous and which were not. Everyone got a chance to hold them, to realize that if you're gentle with them, they won't snap back.

At one point, Dooley said, the various cages and aquariums in the room housed two hundred snakes, and with so many came catastrophes. During one school holiday, a Congo eel slid out of its aquarium and wiggled into the heating system. "We had to fish him out piece by piece with a coat hanger, cause the smell was just . . ." The tale of the water moccasin and the rat snake ended similarly.

The two were housed in a large aquarium built into the outer wall of the classroom, so passersby could view it. Over Easter break, the moccasin killed the rat snake, precipitating "a rotting process in water and on land" that stunk up the whole school.

For another unit, the students had to acquire a freshly killed bird, fish, or mammal, skin it, cook the meat off the bones at home, bring the bones to class, reassemble the skeletons, and mount them on a display board. "There was no way I knew what bone went where," Dooley said. "So if it looked like the wing up there was not a foot, the kids got a passing grade. And I could hear them talking: 'We don't know where these bones go—we just glued them—and he doesn't know the difference.'"

This assignment, too, generated problems. One morning, a boy walked in late, bearing four-footed roadkill. "Mr. Dooley, I found my thing!" the kid hollered, and Dooley waved him to the makeshift stove in the back of the room, where a pressure cooker awaited those whose parents didn't appreciate the "home cooking" part of the assignment.

Dooley continued his lecture until the pressure cooker steamed. "But the steam didn't rise," he said. "It dripped over the pot and started moving toward the floor just like when the Angel of Death came to the Egyptians."

A sour stench quickly enveloped the room. Dooley asked the perpetrator how fresh the roadkill was, and the boy replied, 'I don't know—it had flies and everything.'"

Within seconds, the pressure cooker went flying out the classroom door into a ditch.

Then there was the live chicken Julie Hebert brought to class in a tow sack, for the same assignment. Dooley asked her if she wanted him to "take care of" her chicken, and Julie, looking a bit uneasy, asked what he meant.

"I said, 'We'll we have to cut the neck and bleed the chicken, and then skin it, and then we're going to boil the meat off.' Julie started crying. 'You're not going to do this, Mr. Dooley!" she wailed. "My chicken has a bad leg, and you can't do this to a chicken with a bad leg!'"

The chicken remained in the sack all day, hobbling around within, and finally Dooley said, "Julie, the whole idea is to get something dead and work on the bones. Take your chicken home and bring in a catfish or a perch."

Earl recalled another part of the carcass project: the boiling of the skulls. He and a classmate named Katie had been assigned to "take care of" the heads once attached to the raccoons, squirrels, possums, and other skeletons the kids had hauled in. Dooley planned to arrange the cleaned craniums and mandibles on a table for an identification test.

"Katie lived about a block away from me," Earl said, "so we decided to boil the skulls in a crawfish boiler in her driveway. One day a guy from across the street came over and asked what we were cooking, and we told him, 'Head stew!' We pulled the lid off and the guy looked in and saw all those heads bobbing around—he didn't know what to make of it. We told him it was an assignment from Mr. Dooley."

For botany, Dooley was allowed to take his charges out into the field once a week, often borrowing time from other classes. Kids with cars or trucks drove everyone to the field or swamp Dooley had selected, and they'd set to work, identifying and gathering species—hundreds of them. Several times, the class was granted the entire day to traverse far reaches of the parish. Once they drove to Cote Blanche, the island in the coastal marsh by Vermillion Bay, not far from the islands Earl once hunted for rabbits. Cote Blanche contains a commercially mined salt dome, and at the time, a visit required special permission and a ferry ride to the property. Earl remembered Cote Blanche as "a wonderland of mysterious ravines, weird plants, and mosquito hawks with a foot-long wingspan."

"There was a lot of cross-pollination going on along the Gulf," he said. "I saw a pine tree growing out of an oak. And the soil produced palmettos that were ten, twelve feet tall. It was like Jurassic Park." Dooley remembered squads of armadillos, and the students who chased them around the island.

Both Dooley and Earl recall the tasting of the elephant ear root, an exercise Dooley's biology professor in Monroe had used to teach students about oxalic acid in plants. The elephant ear root can be cooked down to make an edible paste, but tasted raw, laced with its natural dose of oxalic acid, it produces a temporary, but sizzling burn in the mouth—

the plant's defense against predators. A big bite can be poisonous. After explaining the conditions, Dooley invited Earl to take a little bite of the root, as he had done under his teacher. "It was passed down to me, so I passed it down to him," he said.

Earl did more than taste—he ate the whole root. "It was like thousands of razor blades in my mouth," he said. Sickened, he retched into the weeds. Later he decided it was a fitting reaction to an invasive species (from Southeast Asia and Polynesia).

The next unit, the digestive system, required no field trips, to Earl's relief. Last came six weeks on genetics, and six on evolution. Dooley assured the students that this final subject would not interfere with their religious beliefs. "I'm just going to teach you what's being taught out there," he told them, "because we have to have an answer for dinosaurs." A parent complained, though, and Dooley decided not to assign grades for that unit.

* * *

Randy Dooley left Berwick High after three and a half years and went to work for his father's shrimp-processing business, making even less money than he had as a teacher. By 1975, he'd had enough of his tightfisted father and the stink of shrimp. The Watergate scandal and President Nixon's resignation had shaken his confidence in the future, and like any other disgruntled young man, he needed to get the hell out of Dodge. So he moved to France, where he imagined "life is sophisticated, and they don't have a sick economy and a president hated by the world." A year later, having attended classes at the Sorbonne, dallied in the Louvre, and spoken French on the streets, Dooley was back at his parents' home in Delcambre, broke. He valued his experience but was also "thrilled to death that I was from Louisiana, whether the rest of the United States cared about us or not. I was happy to be home, happy to be with people who were so different."

The story doesn't end there, though. Dooley, still under his father's thumb, was back running the shrimp plant at all hours and getting nowhere. One night he staged a dramatic escape: friends pulled his packed belongings from his bedroom window, and the next morning at breakfast with his parents, Dooley announced he was leaving for Houston. And it was more complicated than that: he had bought a plane ticket to Guadalajara, where he enrolled in an intensive Spanish course.

Dooley stayed in Mexico to attend medical school, paid for with seasonal earnings at the shrimp plant, after his father begrudgingly agreed to it. After completing a residency in internal medicine in New York City and another in obstetrics/gynecology in Texas, he returned to Louisiana the second time. A hospital in Morgan City had asked him to come, specifically because he had taught across the river years before and knew the community—an important qualification in Louisiana. Randy Dooley decided to open a private practice there, instead. At forty, he was home for good.

Over his eighteen years as a local doctor, Dooley ran into many members of Earl's advanced biology class. And even though he has based his retirement life in quiet Patterson, fitting his home with beautiful, historically accurate carpets and wallpapers, he still glows, recalling his untamed stint at Berwick High.

"I had eighteen of you for two years, an hour a day, and still, every time I get together with somebody from that class, another set of memories comes up," he told Earl and me, as he refilled our china cups. "I had to expend so much energy just to keep you interested, but it was a really good time. And I'm the one who came out well. Y'all met only one of me. But I met all of y'all."

Music

Earl may have had an early environmental mentor in Randy Dooley, but he wasn't so lucky in music—he would wait a few years for that. Instead, he got into performing by playing and improvising with friends. It all started in the fifth grade, when he and David Burke, his classmate and next-door neighbor, listened to the high school drum line practice in the stadium nearby and grew enamored of rhythm. David had a snare drum at home, and the friends stood together over it, duplicating what they'd heard. In the sixth grade, the pair signed up to play drums in the beginning band, but Earl was forced by the band director to take up the trombone—"a necessary evil," he calls it—probably to ensure the brass section was filled. Burke, who today works as a deputy clerk for the Fulton County (Georgia) government and composes Christian music, remembered that he and Earl were "very influenced by the Beatles." He, Earl, and a trumpet-playing pal formed a combo, working out tunes like "The Saints" by ear. All three boys knew the New Orleans street band classics—their families took them to Mardi Gras every year.

"Earl really took off quickly on the trombone," Burke told me. "He was considerably better than the others. The band director recognized him at one concert as one of the exceptional musicians in the band, but he was exceptional to all of us."

Earl and David continued to play trombone and drum duets together, as David now had a full drum set, and Earl finally talked Adam and Eula into giving him a drum set, too. David remembered it was a nice one—pearly white. By now David had learned the guitar and would bring it over to Earl's house. "I'd play a few chords, and Earl would jam on the drums, or he'd sing."

He also remembered that Earl's parents sometimes put the kibosh on their activities. "They were kind of strict—they protected him," he said. "They made him take a nap when I wasn't taking naps anymore. And his mom would feed us so much food."

"I never saw Earl get mad, but I have seen his feelings get hurt. He was always kind, friendly, and very creative." And independent, too. "One time he strapped a drum to his belly and walked through the neighborhood playing it, all by himself."

Earl considered himself a drummer, despite his facility on the trombone.

"I'd come home from band practice and play the drums," Earl said, in response to David's memories. "I saw two ways to approach the drum set: through standard percussion rudiments, or learned patterns, from the military; or through the cadence, which is built on question and answer, or cause and effect. I took the second approach, the one jazz drummers use. It's more musical—it's all about phrasing. That's what led to composing—portioning out rhythmic time."

* * *

By age fourteen, Earl had eased away from Eula's watch, making extended summer excursions by bus or train to see his Thibodeaux cousins in Port Arthur, Texas, part of the Beaumont–Port Arthur–Orange "Golden Triangle," where many Louisianans had migrated to work the oil fields. Southeast Texas' rice fields, railroad, and shrimp industries also attracted those who would escape their home state's weak economy, whether post–Civil War, or last year.

In that dank corner of Texas, music flourished. Earl's uncle Raymond Thibodeaux, a professional trumpet player, had studied with Harry James's father, a longtime Beaumont resident, and Raymond's children had been taught big-band music and other tunes on various instruments. Pam, the oldest daughter, played keyboard and sang. Patricia played drums, and Peggy sang. Ray Jr. played guitar and bass. Earl, drumsticks in hand, fit right in, sometimes staying in Port Arthur the entire summer to play in his cousins' band. Jamming all night two hundred miles from home provided Earl "a new kind of freedom." The band had real gigs, too—at fairs, in high school gyms, fire stations, and clubs, booked and supervised by Earl's aunt Jerri. Earl was astonished by their audiences.

"I was used to kids who pretty much got along well, and schools that had no fighting," he says. "In the world of Port Arthur, there were rednecks, and Hispanic girls who had knife fights. It was almost so foreign I couldn't take it seriously. In some of the places my cousins and I played, they had nets to protect you from the bottles."

The band departed from old standards, covering Jimi Hendrix, Cream, and the Allman Brothers.

"This is when I really got serious about music. Ray introduced me to Hendrix and Johnny Winter, and I listened to those guys a lot. I didn't consider that music as entertainment."

Winter, a Beaumont local, released his first album, *Progressive Blues Experiment,* on an Austin label in 1968 the summer Earl turned fourteen. Uncle Raymond had first heard Johnny and Edgar Winter in local clubs, for a fifty-cent cover charge. "He told me rednecks would wait until they were finished playing and beat them up on the outside, just because they looked different," Earl says.

Janis Joplin was around, too—in spirit, anyway. The Port Arthur native had already made her mark nationally with Big Brother and the Holding Company, but Earl's cousin Pam, three years older than he, had gone to high school with Joplin and remembered her well. "Pam told me she dressed really weird, and nobody associated with her," Earl said, bearing out similar stories. The idea that Joplin, an overweight be-pimpled misfit, and the Winter brothers, both born with albinism, all made it artistically, impressed Earl. "Out of the mud grows the lily," he says. Later on, Earl would be drawn to the work of neo-Dada artist Robert Rauschenberg, also a Port Arthur native.

The music scene in Beaumont–Port Arthur raised Earl's sights and also provided some personal validation. One night, when the cousins were jamming, a couple of musicians with a dobro and a bass dropped in. Aunt Jerri took one look at their ravaged physiques and said, "It's fine with me if you all play music with them, but I can tell they're on hard drugs, like heroin."

The jam session went on, Earl holding down the rhythm. Afterward, the two visitors asked him to join their band. "But I was in the eighth grade. I told them I had to get back to school." Cousin Ray was incredulous: "Do you realize what you just turned down? Those guys play all over the place!" The two musicians' names are long forgotten, but Earl remembers how he felt after that night. "Just the knowledge that I was good enough to be in their band was a confirmation that I was serious enough to make it, in their ears. Much better than getting little medals for playing crummy march music on the trombone."

In any local mix of musically talented teens, perhaps one or two will continue training and performing after high school. Some fire hotter than natural ability has been lit, and the young man or woman, bowing to desire or destiny, will do anything to keep fanning the flames. There's no turning back, one realizes, and how come everybody else doesn't feel the same way? Earl says that, to his cousins, music was only a passing fad. "They got into the world of making money for their families. They look at me as the guy who was naïve enough to believe I could make it as a musician. They just didn't understand."

Back in Berwick, Earl bought his own Jimi Hendrix and Cream albums, listened obsessively to drummers Mitch Mitchell and Ginger Baker, and worked out their riffs in the living room while ten feet away in the kitchen, Eula sighed and stirred gumbo.

"I felt then that I just had to get the hell out of here," he says.

                                  . . . .

In fall 1972, Earl entered LSU as a trombonist in the Tiger band with no declared major, and learned it was one thing to dream about becoming Mitch Mitchell, another to be the first in his family to confront the many choices squeezed into a college catalogue. During his weekends at home, Adam and Eula, who had no notion of the freshman experience, quizzed him anxiously: what was he going to do? "I wrung myself out, trying to get onto a career path—I literally memorized the curriculum for anything I might want to do—like to be a forestry major, an agronomist, anything. It went on and on. Finally, I just said, enough! I'm here to learn and take classes I want to take, and I'll deal with the other stuff later."

Earl declared himself a biology major, perhaps to follow Randy Dooley as a teacher, but by summer decided to apply to the music composition program. "One thing led to another," he says. "I hung out a lot with a guy in architecture who had a huge record collection. He had worked at Discount Records in Houston and had apple crates of everything from the thirteenth-century Notre Dame School to John Cage. We would spend hours listening."

Earl presented himself to the music department's audition committee, aware that he might not meet their standards. For all of his inborn talent, his "legit" preparation in the Berwick band had been limited. He didn't know all of his scales on the trombone and had no formal background in music theory. The biggest hurdle lay with Juilliard-trained members in the piano area, who were to evaluate his keyboard skills. Earl, the drummer who would be part of the Jimi Hendrix Experience, had never touched a piano.

"The chair said, 'What are you going to play for us?' And I said, 'I don't play. I want to take piano because I'm in composition.' And he said, 'What about a scale?' And I said, 'I don't play anything—I don't know anything about the piano.' And he said, 'Well, can you find middle C?' And I said, 'No.'"

After the predictable round of raised eyebrows, throat clearings, and an administrative scuffle over whether Earl was required to take four years of piano (he was not), the faculty assigned him to a group piano course. Earl found the piano easy to play. Three months later, he played a performance exam for the same pianists who'd frowned on him at the start of the term. When he finished, the committee chair asked if he was sure he'd never played the piano before. "And I said no, not before this semester." The chair didn't buy it, arguing that it was impossible for Earl to have adapted so well to the keyboard in so short a time. "I was totally relaxed," Earl said. "He couldn't believe it. First they gave me a hard time because I didn't know anything; then they gave me a hard time because I did."

It turned out that Earl was a natural pianist, a welcome gift to the composer who manipulates harmony by sounding it out. Still, he is most grateful for his early experience as a rhythm man. "Harmony can be taught," he said, the day we spoke of this in the Robicheaux house living room, "but without an internal sense of rhythm and proportion, without a way of expressing ideas rhythmically, you're not going to have much."

By this time, Earl had made peace with the idea that a degree in music composition would not guarantee a career, or even a job. Adam was not so relaxed. He threw up his hands, warning Earl that he'd soon be on his own. Eula worried, too, but took solace in a comment from Earl's high school chemistry teacher, a customer at Adam's barbershop.

"He told my parents, 'Don't worry about Earl—he's gonna do OK.' So in a weird sort of way, they relied on the opinions of people like Mr. Turner."

Besides playing trombone in the LSU band and orchestra, Earl jammed on drums with friends who played guitar and bass. It kept him sane, he says, in a place that in the early 1970s failed to recognize one of his heroes, John Cage, philosophically probably the most audacious American composer of the century and a champion of pieces made from natural, or ambient, sounds. One might say Cage was a master at setting up the conditions for such pieces—inviting or encouraging them. A signature work, *4:33*, calls for a pianist to stride onstage, position herself on the bench, sit silently for exactly four minutes and thirty-three seconds, then walk off. The music is the ambient sound contained in that time: rattling programs, random sneezes, an air-conditioning system cycling on and off. Earl remembers being called to a meeting with the head of the brass faculty, and told to consider dropping out of the program, specifically for his interest in Cage. Earl refused.

LSU's cold climate for new music warmed for Earl when the Yugoslavian conductor/composer Konstantin Simonovitch arrived as a visiting professor. The former director of Ensemble Instrumental de Musique Contemporaine de Paris, at that time the world's premier new music ensemble, Simonovitch had led and recorded works by the century's great innovators, including the French composer Edgar Varèse—sometimes called "The Father of Electronic Music"—whose nonpitched, theatrical, to most ears zany music had once so excited a fifteen-year-old Frank Zappa that the San Diego teen spent his five-dollar birthday money on a phone call to Varèse in New York. Another of Simonovitch's composers was Luc Ferrari, a Varèse devotee, also French, who explored abstract and conceptual art through *musique concrète:* electronic and acoustic music employing sounds beyond those achievable by conventional voices and instruments.

Luc Ferrari was, artistically speaking, a free spirit. You cannot fingerprint him like Mozart or Beethoven. Some of his instrumental

music comes across as improvisatory collections of events and gestures—
sporadic vocals, evocative drummings, keyboard strikes and more, over-
lapping, occurring simultaneously, or hanging alone like a pendulum
in silence. Other works are more linear, surging toward an end. Then
there are electronic pieces like *Les Anecdotiques,* which would inform Earl
years later, when he began composing Atchafalaya Basin soundscapes.
Les Anecdotiques comprises three simultaneous planes: a sequence from
sounds in a place the composer had visited (from Tuscany to Texas),
abstract electronic sounds, and snippets of interviews with young women.
The music's physical qualities, like objects or worlds colliding in space,
evoke the controlled chaos of nature.

"He combined an inner world and an outer world," Earl says. "He
was interested in the psychology of how we listen. Eventually, we realize
the inner and outer are one. It's like Buddhist awareness."

Sounds and processes in nature influenced Luc Ferrari, and you can
hear it in the repeated patterns and backgrounds that change almost
imperceptibly, like leaves turning in autumn. Birdcalls and songs occasionally figured in his work, but not as much as for Olivier Messiaen,
another eminent Frenchman Simonovitch championed. An amateur
ornithologist, Messiaen roamed the French countryside recording birds,
then notated them on a musical staff and planted them in his works, creating one of the twentieth century's most distinctive musical languages.

I've played some of his pieces on the clarinet—delighted to imitate
the wood thrush, the lark, the prairie chicken.

Earl already knew music by these composers and was captured completely by Simonovitch.

"He was so radical compared to anyone or anything else in Louisiana," Earl said. "I remember, he had striped pants and frizzed-out hair,
and he looked like a clown. He played four or five instruments. I put it
together, how big this guy was. We became instant friends."

Earl became Simonovitch's assistant for the year and a regular at the
conductor's house, where he got to know Simonovitch's wife, Arlette
Sibon-Simonovitch, an expert on the *ondes Martinot,* an early French

electronic instrument with an eerie, oscillating voice. A few years later, when Simonovitch had moved to New York and Earl to Washington, D.C., Earl took the bus up to see him several times.

"We'd stay up nights, looking at scores, and listening to recordings," Earl said. "He always referred to me as 'the young composer from Louisiana.' Getting to know him was pivotal for me. He represented all the things I thought had to be out there and hadn't experienced—New York and Paris combined."

Under Simonovitch's guidance at LSU Earl made his first electronic piece, *Attack of the Giant Frog Chorus,* composed on an early Moog synthesizer. The drones and croaks are entirely faux. "Even though I didn't consciously understand it, those sounds had always been in my ear," Earl says. In the university's electronic studio, he synthesized four different frog groups, generating tapes in a four-channel mix. By using four loudspeakers, each with its own sound source, Earl was able to place frog groups in various locations in a concert hall. This way, he could achieve location modulation—that is, he could merge two or more sound groups within the overall space and create the effect of standing in the middle of a swamp, listening to frogs from all sides. Overall, Earl's frog pods pulled off some complex rhythmic phasing: a cyclical process that happens when two or more voices (or groups of voices), singing in unison rhythm, depart from one another, swing "out of sync," and eventually reunite. (In classic phasing, there is one constant "axis" voice, from which the others depart, and to which they return.)

"The effects of convergence and divergence between groups of callers reflect one of the most primary aspects of nature," Earl says. "It's the unfolding of time."

Later, in a sociopolitical gesture, he wrote *Notice the Wall to the Right,* a piece for a narrator whose face was painted half black, half white, and a blues ensemble of students from LSU and Southern University, a traditionally black school in Baton Rouge. The prepared tape recorder, placed onstage in a manger, played a French conversation running backward, and, like other electroacoustic works from that time, confronted the narrator with the problem of who ruled the roost. The narrator ran screaming from the stage, and the musicians closed the show with a dark blues number. Earl admits that, as a student work, *Notice the Wall to the Right* was a bit heavy on the symbolism, but it got him thinking about uses for taped voices.

After Simonovitch left LSU, the American experimental composer James Drew arrived as a guest. Drew was keen on Cage and his followers, working with "chance" music, where the work's outcome depends on some degree of randomness. Before coming to Baton Rouge, he taught at Yale and played with musicians like John Coltrane at the Village Vanguard. He would later make inroads in radio theater, music notation, and sound installations.

Now in his eighties, Drew describes the LSU School of Music in the 1970s as "sort of archaic. I finally resigned because I was actually told I was making certain faculty members uncomfortable because I was getting performed throughout the world, and they weren't, and that made them feel bad. I said, 'I'm sorry about that; it's out of my hands. I can only do what I do.'"

During his short tenure at LSU, Drew taught a few students in his home studio. Earl was among them, and Drew remembers "someone who was intelligent enough to know they weren't learning anything in that environment. Most enjoyable about him was a thirst for knowledge."

Drew guided Earl's composing, warning him against a typical beginner's problem: writing too fast, failing to allow intellectual, psychological, and technical aspects to deepen their way to a satisfying piece. The two kicked back for conversation, too, but not always about music per se. Mainly, Drew says, they chewed on ideas, like the ties between developing technology and a possible parallel human decline—a perennial fear that surfaces every time a technological leap is made, and that many artists, including those who make use of those leaps, are compelled to examine.

Earl's high school and college years coincided with the rise of the modern environmental movement, spearheaded by books like Rachel Carson's *Silent Spring* and Paul Ehrlich's *The Population Bomb*. Several

environmental catastrophes in the 1960s contributed to growing awareness, among them a 1969 offshore oil spill from a well in Santa Barbara
Channel, California, that caught Earl's and other south Louisianans' attention. The year 1969 also saw the *Apollo 11* moon landing and astronaut
Neil Armstrong's first steps on the desolate surface. This was my own
watershed event. I had just finished high school in Titusville, a Florida
Space Coast town, and remember camping the night before the launch
with friends à la Woodstock on the Indian River across from NASA
Launch Complex A, surrounded by thousands of visitors from all over
the country. My interest in humans' relationship to nature arose then,
not simply as an add-on to my mother's legacy as an outdoorswoman but
in response to the enormous symbol of that launching pad, about three
miles from the wild beach I had strolled with my transistor radio. (The
pad and the beach lay adjacent to what later became the Merritt Island
Wildlife Refuge—land bought by the government as a barrier for Cape
Kennedy and inadvertently protected.) That summer even affected my
father, an amateur poet who, forty years before, escaped his family's Indiana farm one night to ride the rails toward work as a traveling salesman
and eventually made it as a white-collar manager. After the *Apollo 11*
moon landing, he suddenly spoke of returning to the farm at retirement,
comforted by the thought of harvesting wheat.

In 1970, President Nixon proposed and signed into law the Environmental Protection Agency, and soon after, the government passed
supporting legislation such as the Federal Water Pollution Control
Amendments of 1972 (soon strengthened as the Clean Water Act of
1977) and the Endangered Species Act (1973). An earlier piece of pro-
environment legislation, the National Environmental Policy Act of 1969,
included a new acronym: EIS, or environmental impact statement, a
requirement that gave environmental activists something to work with
and would later trouble the Thibodeaux property on Bayou Boeuf, which
Jim Thibodeaux had leased to an oil-fabrication company in 1960.

Earl wasn't aware of the property's increasingly precarious state. To
him, it was still his family's place, and after he turned sixteen in 1970

and got his driver's license, he started taking pals to the "big house" late at night to sit on the porch, drink wine, and conjure spooky Aunt Ida as the bayou glided toward the Gulf. By then, the old people had died, and the place was empty and deteriorating under the relaxed eye of a caretaker living in a trailer nearby. Under a full moon, it offered a kind of creepy beauty.

But in spring 1973, his sophomore year at LSU, Earl took a serious ride on a Greyhound bus, traveling home during the great Mississippi flood. The high backwaters between Thibodaux and Morgan City alarmed him, he says, but not as much as the sight of the Atchafalaya nearly topping the seawall. He remembers walking out on the old train bridge to watch the water whiz by. It raced so fast he couldn't keep track of the whirlpools that quickly formed bigger whirlpools, "and gave the optical illusion that the bridge I was standing on was flying."

• • •

The 1973 flood, the most severe on the lower Mississippi since 1927, nearly caused the Old River Control Structure to fail. Experts agreed the flood was human-made; the constricted system gave the spring waters no place to go but straight down the navigation chute, resulting in high levels the levees couldn't control. In December, the Flood Disaster Protection Act of 1973 was put into effect, expanding the national flood insurance program and requiring flood-prone communities to participate in it. Those in south Louisiana without flood insurance signed up.

In 1975, when he was a senior at LSU, Earl heard about a proposal that would send the Army Corps of Engineers to dredge Bayous Chene, Black, and Boeuf, in order to speed oil jacks to the Gulf. The proposal was still pending approval in 1977, when Earl, age twenty-three, with a bachelor of music in hand, was back in Berwick, living at home and working as a night dispatcher for Delta Mud, a company that supplied drilling mud and chemicals to oil rigs. Having a personal interest in Bayou Boeuf, and certain the dredging would kill the bayou oyster beds, Earl drew up and circulated a petition among fishermen, calling for a stop to the project. He surprised himself a little with his activism—as a drummer, he was used to the back of the stage, and as a composer, to the back of the hall. He described a public meeting on the issue: "Two biologists from LSU, and some businessmen, laughing at the biologists." Earl himself presented a paper on ways dredging would affect the Barataria-Terrebonne estuary. "It would have meant draining a parish that feeds a lot of people," Earl said. The project was approved anyway, then vetoed by President Carter, and as Earl expected, the veto was eventually overridden. But in place of the original project, the Army Corps dredged a different canal.

"Even though they went ahead, I learned that one voice can make a difference," Earl said. "I wouldn't view myself at that time as an ecologist, but I was going against the grain. In my unconscious, I felt my father's world was under threat."

Earl was already going against the grain at Delta Mud; it's safe to say he was the only employee in the company's history to bring Schoenberg's Violin Concerto to study on nights when the phone and radio didn't offer much action. "I had a lot of time to twiddle my thumbs," he admits. He continued to study modernist composers and delved further into Renaissance music. His schedule dictated fourteen days on and five days off, and on the days off he drove to New Orleans to order more scores. He remembers when River Books on Uptown Square went out of business, and how he laid in a huge supply of music then.

Earl stayed at Delta Mud for nearly two years. During that time, he received his first commission, a big-band piece titled *Parodies Parable* for Music for Musicians in collaboration with New Orleans Jazz and Heritage Festival founder George Wein and producer Quint Davis. It was premiered at the festival in 1978.

Here, my life nearly intersected with Earl's. I was living in New Orleans then, fresh from graduate school in Michigan, teaching clarinet lessons at Loyola University and giving tours through a historic house in the French Quarter. Sensing Louisiana didn't hold enough suitable musical opportunities for me, I started flying to New York once a month for more private lessons and practiced like a madwoman, preparing to jump to something new, somewhere else. Yet on weekends, I enjoyed driving the river road west, exploring the old plantation lands that led to the Atchafalaya, getting mercifully lost in the byways defining rice fields, cane fields, and the oak-shaded grounds of Catholic churches. I did not attend the Jazz and Heritage Festival when Earl's piece was premiered; it's entirely possible I spent that afternoon rolling along the I-10 bridge over Henderson Swamp.

Earl was on the verge of change, too. Not long after the festival, Delta Mud offered him the opportunity to become a mud engineer. He turned it down and began thinking, as Randy Dooley once had, of finally leaving Louisiana.

CHAPTER 5

Outsider Artist

Faced with a choice between becoming a mud engineer and anything else, Earl Robicheaux embarked on a twenty-year odyssey that took him away from home and back, twice. Like his biology teacher Randy Dooley's two sojourns, one of Earl's trips to "the outside" was short, the other long, and both grew out of the desire for education and a more cosmopolitan experience.

In 1978, after hearing his big-band

piece premiered at the Jazz and Heritage Festival, Earl upped and drove five hundred miles from Berwick to Denton, Texas, attracted by North Texas State University's large music school, known for its world-class jazz program. I had begun studying there during the summers toward a doctorate in clarinet performance, beginning in 1976, and remember well my own reaction, pulling into Denton for the first time, fresh from New Orleans: "There's a great music school *here?*" Compared to Louisiana, north-central Texas was abysmally bereft of greenery, and its sky unsettlingly high and wide. The campus itself, a grid of rectangular buildings all stacked of dust-yellow brick, did not promise a rich world of art making. But inside those plain halls I found a lot to like, and in 1979, left New Orleans permanently to study in Denton, carving a niche in my two years there playing contemporary music.

Although Earl and I overlapped a few months in Denton, we never met, partly because the school is so big, and Earl was somewhat adrift there, anyway. "Denton was one of those blind moves," he said. "It was just time *to* move. And though I went to North Texas because I'd heard of the jazz program, it was not the kind of school I wanted—I was looking for something more academic."

At North Texas, Earl met Kathy Huisman, a pianist from Falls Church, Virginia, and the pair married and moved close to her family in the Washington, D.C., area. Earl and Kathy found office jobs, but a year later, Earl came across C. C. Lockwood's *National Geographic* spread on the Atchafalaya and convinced his new bride to move to Morgan City.

Earl speaks fondly of his time in D.C.'s museums as a crash course in contemporary visual art that would inform his music, and ultimately, his approach to recording sounds in the Atchafalaya. The New York School abstract expressionists, and Robert Rauschenberg in particular, caught his attention. "I could relate to Rauschenberg through my own experience," he said, "because he was from Port Arthur. But more than that was the work—the idea that you could make meaning out of nonmeaning. Rauschenberg would give himself a rule—like, any object he found within, say, one block, could be part of a work. There was a sense for the moment—it had a Buddhist aspect to it." It also mirrored the Cageian aesthetic, and the freedom of the unconscious mind prized by all disciples of the New York School—writers, musicians, dancers, visual artists.

The abstract expressionists particularly suggested to Earl, as they had for many other composers, the idea of writing pieces for the sake of pure color or for groups or nests or planes of sounds. These concepts became more interesting to Earl than conventional relationships between pitch and harmony. He also began thinking about synthesizing traditional music and "found" objects (or to put it musically, in random or captured sounds).

"And that led to an interest in the natural world," Earl said, "because in nature, there is no square or rectangle. Yet man bases all of his architecture and common practices of music on the rectangle or square. In music, Varèse had broken through that."

Looking to Marcel Duchamp also provided food for thought. "He showed that here could be poetry in the relationships between objects, and so did Joseph Cornell. What I'm trying to do now is the equivalent in sound—where everyday sounds are put into a context from which a kind of poetry can emerge."

⋅   ⋅   ⋅

Earl's first full year back in Louisiana, 1981, was marked by a personal tragedy that would shape and shadow the rest of his life. Adam Robicheaux, who had suffered a stroke in 1975, died of another, at home. That winter, Earl and his wife were living in a garage apartment attached to the Robicheaux Street place. In the main house one day, Adam drew a bath for himself, leaving the bathroom's gas wall heater on, and asked Earl to check on him in a while. Sometime later, Eula discovered her husband, lifeless, in the tub. Earl blames himself for forgetting to check on his father and the heat delivered by the wall unit, though he knows it's impossible to say what brought on his father's stroke. Adam's health had been compromised much earlier by an alcohol problem, "two beers when he came home from work, and more on the weekends," according to Earl, and his half sister Carolyn confirms alcoholism led to the breakup of Adam's first marriage. Earl's sorrow over his father's death can be measured by his minimal commentary on the event. "I try not to think about it," he says, and will not go further. Adam's life was commemorated two blocks from the Atchafalaya River in a Mass at St. Stephen Catholic Church in Berwick, where Earl had served as an altar boy. Earl read a prepared statement, and his wife played special organ music, including an arrangement of a violin and organ piece Earl had written for their marriage, and a work by Pachelbel. "A lot of people came because he was a fixture in the town," Earl said.

In 1981 and 1982, Earl worked as a compositor's apprentice at King-Hannaford, the printing company in Morgan City where Eula had once worked, and at the same time, resumed studying composing with James Drew, who had left LSU but remained in the New Orleans area. In 1983, Earl and his wife moved to New Orleans, and he found a job with a printing company in Kenner. But soon after that, the young couple divorced ("We were young," Earl says), and Earl began a relationship with a Loyola University music student, Vickie Robertson, who would be his partner for the next twelve years.

Vickie and Earl met while they were working at Leisure Landing, a record store on Magazine Street I remember well. A no-frills barn of a place, on a typical Magazine Street block, containing, as I recall, a Popeye's chicken, an antiques shop, an oyster bar, and a laundromat, Leisure Landing had opened in 1978, my last full year in New Orleans. I benefited from the store's arrival after it hired away the classical buyer from the hippie-run Mushroom Records near Tulane, leaving a vacancy that I, who had just left my eight-to-five job at the historic house in the French Quarter, conveniently slipped into. For the next nine months, I ministered to the symphony and opera lovers who still dared to creep past Mushroom's prominent head shop to request the latest *Tosca* or *Bolero*.

For their first date, Earl and Vickie attended a concert of music by Sandy Hinderlie, a friend of mine from North Texas days who had joined the Loyola University music faculty in 1981. Though the paper programs no longer exist, several of us are reasonably sure that was the night I appeared at Loyola as Sandy's guest artist, along with former North Texas colleagues Karen Ray (a cellist married to Sandy at the time) and Therese Costes, a soprano whom Sandy had also invited to fly in. A percussionist and two more keyboard and synthesizer jocks rounded out the personnel. Earl remembers Sandy's electronic equipment banked across the stage "like a *Star Wars* set." I played my heart out that night, inspired by Sandy's music and my adventurous friends.

When Vickie described for me her six years with Earl in New Orleans, she brought back the way the city felt when I lived there: so easygoing I had time to take the pokey St. Charles Avenue streetcar most anywhere I needed to be, leaning back in my wooden seat, savoring the breeze from the open windows as if I were on vacation.

"We led a typical New Orleans life," Vickie told me on the phone one night from Houston, where she lives now. "You know—hanging out with friends, eating seafood." The couple rented a two-bedroom house uptown at the corner of Pitt and Pine, in a typical mixed-race neighborhood four blocks from Audubon Park and the Mississippi River. Because the only air conditioner in the house was a window unit in the sleeping bedroom, they kept the windows open and "could hear all of our neighbors' business." The other bedroom was Earl's studio, frequented by his beloved cat, Mingus, who commanded a perch atop the piano. One day when Earl wasn't there, Vickie said, she put some Debussy piano music on the record player, and Mingus jumped to the keyboard and walked up and down, creating his own musical impressionism.

Earl and Vickie's house at Pitt and Pine was not far from my former home, a tiny shotgun on Panola Street, near Tulane and Loyola. After I moved into it, I spent two months clearing the jungle the previous owner had allowed the backyard to become. When I finally tore away that gargantuan kudzu tent, I discovered three dozen trash bags filled with discarded kitty litter, several hundred pounds of disintegrating garbage, and two promising fruit trees: fig and loquat. My next-door neighbor, who worked on oil rigs in the Gulf, ten days on, ten days off, said he'd never seen anyone drag so many Hefty bags to the curb. The fig and loquat survived and bore fruit; I planted a white camellia between them. It was then that my expeditions to rural south Louisiana began, as if, in thrashing about in my overgrown yard I had survived an initiation ritual, like the eating of an elephant ear root.

Earl admits that he was work-averse in New Orleans, moving among jobs at various printing companies. But he never had a problem getting work; by now, he was handling all prepress composition: layout and design, typesetting, drawing forms on a light table, producing and stripping negatives in a darkroom, proofreading, and so on. At one job, a chance encounter brought full circle the *National Geographic* story of basin dwellers Gwen Roland and Calvin Voisin, which had inspired Earl to return home a few years before. One day, from his workspace adjacent to the noisy pressroom, he noticed a familiar-looking man repairing a huge Heidelberg press. He couldn't recall where he'd seen the fellow and finally approached him on a hunch. "You wouldn't know the photographer C. C. Lockwood, would you?" And Calvin Voisin replied, "Yes, and that article cost me my life, man."

It turned out that the *National Geographic* piece had revealed Voisin's seasonal occupation as a crawfisherman, inviting the Internal Revenue Service to check his returns. (By then, to meet their need for cash, Gwen had left the basin for a job cooking on a riverboat. More work as a river cook and writer followed, and in time, she met and married a riverboat engineer.) When the IRS discovered Voisin hadn't reported his full income, it claimed his boat. Now, like Gwen, like so many others who had vowed to make it work in the basin, Calvin was making his living on dry ground.

Many years later, in 2007, I met Gwen after her book, *Atchafalaya Houseboat*, was published by the University Press of Mississippi, and PBS was about to reunite Gwen and Calvin for a documentary. In 2009, Gwen said Calvin, sixty-three, was still living at his parents' old place near the Bayou Sorrel Bridge, where she and Calvin had built their houseboat before towing it into the basin. "He has managed to snag one of the only jobs in Bayou Sorrel, tending the bridge," she wrote in an e-mail, noting that bridge tending offers generous reading time. Calvin had just phoned her to recommend a new author. "He works seven days on and seven days off, so he has plenty of time to fish at his little camp boat."

The printer Earl stayed with the longest served the racetrack, and he looked forward every spring to the end of the racing season, collecting unemployment, composing, and going fishing. Vickie said, "I think Earl hated pretty much every job he ever had. Most 'jobs' are pretty creativity-less—at least at the level at which Earl creates. I think the periods he spent living on unemployment were about recovery. And about dreading the next bout of tedium.

"He would sit in the tub for a half hour or so pretty much every day," she recalled. "He often had lower back pain, and this was 'why' he'd sit there. But I wonder if it didn't have something to do with the 'water' at his emotional center, a sort of medium for his own 'vibration' to be supported in, to move through. I think it was a sort of thinking spot."

An astrology buff, Vickie wondered if Earl suffered from "Leo laziness" or depression. "While his music is very carefully ordered, his space was always so littered with clothes, music, paper, books—there was typically no order to be found surrounding his person. It used to drive me crazy. I'd have to make him get out of bed to help me make the bed. He hated that. He once told me (resentfully) as he was getting up to do this that I was obsessed with order. I'm a Virgo, after all.

"It was also hard to get him to exercise. I love to hike, and so we'd go for walks. We lived a few blocks from Audubon Park, and in the winter we'd walk over to the hot house to try to get warm. Earl was always on the lookout for a place to sit down."

⸱ ⸱ ⸱

I can't resist opening Earl's—and the basin's—story to reflections by the author Lafcadio Hearn (1850–1904), who, though best known for his later writings on Japanese culture, spent roughly ten years based in New Orleans, from 1877 to 1888, working as a journalist and maintaining rich correspondence with friends in the north. Excerpts from three letters to Henry Edward Krehbiel, music editor of the *New York Tribune*, capture not only Hearn's florescent style but the ambivalence an artist may feel toward living a creative life in south Louisiana.

In this first letter, Hearn complains about lethargy, then admits he appreciates the interiority his new environment encourages.

New Orleans, 1878

I have really given up all hope of creating anything while I remain here, or, indeed, until my condition shall have altered and my occupation changed.

What material I can glean here, from this beautiful and legendary land,—this land of perfume and dreams,—must be chiseled into shape elsewhere.

One cannot write of these beautiful things while surrounded by them; and by an atmosphere, heavy and drowsy as that of a conservatory. It must be afterward, in times to come, when I shall find myself in some cold, bleak land where I shall dream regretfully of the graceful palms; the swamp groves, weird in their ragged robes of moss; the golden ripples of cane-fields under the summer wind, and this divine sky—deep and vast and cloudless as Eternity, with its far-off horizon tint of tender green.

I do not wonder the South has produced nothing of literary art. Its beautiful realities fill the imagination to repletion. It is regret and desire and the Spirit of Unrest that provoketh poetry and romance. It is the North, with its mists and fogs, and its gloomy sky haunted by a fantastic and ever-changing panorama of clouds, which is the land of imagination and poetry.

I cannot describe to you the peculiar effect of the summer upon one unacclimated. You feel as though you were breathing a drugged atmosphere, you find the very whites of your eyes turning yellow with biliousness. The least over-indulgence in eating or drinking prostrates you.

. . . But this is a land where one can really enjoy the Inner Life. Every one has an inner life of his own,—which no other eye can see, and

*the great secrets of which are never revealed, although occasionally when
we create something beautiful, we betray a faint glimpse of it—sudden
and brief, as of a door opening and shutting in the night.*

Five years later, Hearn has become acclimated and can't imagine being
anywhere else. (Although he feels he has slowed down, he is actually
writing and publishing a great deal.)

New Orleans, 1883
    *New York has become something appalling to my imagination. . . .
When I think of it, I feel more content with my sunlit marshes,—and
the frogs,—and the gnats,—and the invisible plagues lurking in visible vapours,—and the ancientness,—and the vast languor of the land.
Even our vegetation here, funereally drooping in the great heat, seems to
dream of dead things—to mourn for the death of Pan. After a few years
here the spirit of the land has entered into you,—and the languor of the
place embraces you with an embrace that may not be broken;—thoughts
come slowly, ideas take form sluggishly as shapes of smoke in heavy air;
and a great horror of work and activity and noise and bustle roots itself
within your soul,—I mean brain. Soul = Cerebral Activity = Soul.*

A year later, Hearn confesses he may find it difficult to return to New
York, even for a visit. His mind now cleaves to the South, and he worries
the northern city might disturb it.

New Orleans, 1884
    *Just as soon as this beastly weather changes I'll go to New York,
and hope you'll be able—say in April—to give me a few days' loafing-
time.*
    *I'm afraid, however, I shall have to leave my ideas behind me. I
know I could never squeeze them under or over the Brooklyn Bridge.
Furthermore, I'm afraid the Elevated R.R. cars might run over my
ideas and hurt them. In fact, 'tis only in the vast swamps of the South,*

where the converse of the frogs is even as the roar of a thousand waters,
that my Ideas have room to expand.

· · ·

Vickie Robertson said she and Earl visited Eula in Berwick "all the time"
and theorizes his down moods might have come from guilt Eula "flung
his way," as well as his responsibility over his father's death, coupled with
Catholic guilt. "Suffering often plays a huge role in creativity," Vickie
observed. "Earl has always suffered." On their trips to the basin, Earl
was especially drawn to an area north of Morgan City near Four-Mile
Bayou and Pierre Part, a French-speaking community. "He liked to go
there just to listen," Vickie said. "We also drove out to the Bayou Boeuf
house, and he told me how things had changed since the oil industry
had come in—how the salt water came into the swamp."

In 1985, Earl began practicing meditation at a Japanese dojo in New
Orleans. In time, it wrought a significant change in his life. "I sat for
about three years," he said, "getting up at 5:30 every day—it was real good
training. I learned to open up to each day, to find value in everything." At
the same time, he discovered the music of Toru Takemitsu, an important
and hugely prolific contemporary Japanese composer who, influenced by
Debussy and Messiaen as well as Cage, was writing Western music with
an unmistakable Eastern, nature-inspired sensibility, some incorporating
traditional Japanese instruments. Earl loved Takemitsu's lush harmonies
and "anti-architectural approach" to natural subjects like wind, stones, and
Japanese gardens. The composer's meditations on music, humans, and
nature, translated and included in *Confronting Silence, Selected Writings*
(Fallen Leaf Press, 1994), articulate some of Earl's thoughts on those
subjects. Here is an excerpt from Takemitsu's "People and Trees," which
can also be read as the process by which a piece of music may evolve and
be received.

In a magnificent way trees transform time into space. Geometrically
precise, their inner growth rings gradually expand in time to fill

unlimited space. Their growth from within develops in two directions: roots below, branches and leaves above. To people, branches and leaves seem trivial while roots are fundamental. In undivided action and with a glance toward infinity and eternity, leaves create chlorophyll, roots absorb minerals.

So trees exist beyond God's will and human wisdom. Yet the selfishness of humans may destroy them. And that joyful and intimate relationship of people to trees is about to be lost.

Increasingly, Vickie enjoyed watching Earl compose.

"He would sit at the piano working on some current creation, and after working for a time, he'd stop and open a book of Bach pieces—either Anna Magdalena's *Notebook* or the *Well-Tempered Clavier*—I don't remember. He'd start playing, and after a while he'd start improvising, and after a much longer while, 'Do You Know What It Means to Miss New Orleans' would emerge. Literally every time he sat down to the piano, at some point, he'd begin improvising. His fingers moving across the piano made me think of water, trickling, flowing across the keys." As many musicians would attest, ferreting out the harmonic connections between Baroque masters and jazz composers like John Coltrane and Miles Davis is a fine way to develop a harmonic vocabulary.

In the evenings, Earl gigged as a piano soloist in New Orleans restaurants, holding his longest stint at a French Quarter watering hole called Feelings, where he played standards by Cole Porter and Duke Ellington, plus Coltrane "and some Miles." He was paid $150 cash a night plus meals, refusing to put out a tip jar because he didn't want to invite requests for songs he didn't know, and most of the requests came from drunk patrons who wobbled in from Pat O'Brien's, just down the block. Some overimbibed tourists were likely to ask him to sing. "And I don't sing," he said.

But he did compose during this time and produced his first serious pieces, among them one for solo guitar titled *Prajna Rasa*, inspired by his Buddhist studies. It was premiered at Christ Church Cathedral in a recital by guitarist and composer Frank Martinez, whom Earl met at a little shop on Magazine Street that sold instruments from all over the world—Earl hung out there a lot, coveting a set of Congolese log drums. Martinez, who collected exotic instruments, had studied music composition with Louis Andriessen at the Royal Conservatory in the Netherlands, and guitar with Andres Segovia in a master class. Earl worked closely with Martinez for two years. Also at Christ Church, Earl's former wife, Kathy, premiered an organ piece, *Homage to All Souls.*

And Earl continued to accumulate and study recordings. "His recordings were super old, or very new," Vickie Robertson remembered. "He was interested in early music, when composers were discovering how to put it all together, and in new music that was totally out. The great tradition in between that the rest of us preferred was less interesting to him.

"You know, Earl never really felt like he fit into the world. The world is a very superficial place in a lot of ways, and he has never been a superficial kind of person. He used to drive me nuts, he was so critical about ordinary life, possessions, and kitschy things."

•   •   •

One of Earl's favorite artists is the New Orleans–born recluse and Mississippian Walter Inglis Anderson (1903–1965), whose love affair with Horn Island, off the Mississippi coast near Ocean Springs, inspired his thousands of drawings and watercolors as well as significant work in the decorative arts. Anderson came from a wealthy family and trained at the Parsons Institute of Design, New York, and Pennsylvania Academy of Fine Arts in Philadelphia. In 1928, he won an award that enabled him to study in France for a year, where, according to Redding S. Sugg Jr. in his introduction to *The Horn Island Logs of Walter Inglis Anderson,* the young man was unimpressed with the Paris art scene and soon took off for the countryside. On one outing, he came upon the Dordogne River Valley cave paintings. The polychrome animals galloping across the curved limestone walls are rendered in a dark palette (black, red, ochre) and point to the dark palette (black, browns, purple, green) that would come to dominate Anderson's own paintings of Mississippi plants, animals, land, and seascapes.

After his year in France, Anderson settled in Ocean Springs, where his parents had retired to vacation property along the Mississippi Sound. By now, he had read extensively on art history and technique. For a time, he read closely the Greek Armenian mystic G. I. Gurdjieff, who "sought to concentrate in the self the force of nature in order to increase personal power," Sugg wrote, "whereas Anderson sought acceptance by and integration into nature." After his Gurdjieff phase, Anderson was attracted to Adolpho Best-Maugard's *A Method for Creative Design* and James Hambidge's *The Elements of Dynamic Symmetry.* These and other books on his shelves addressed the repeated use of basic motifs found in nature to represent movement—to bring what is represented alive. Their influence is clear in Anderson's work, vibrant with repeated gestures (like curves, waves, straight or wiggly lines) and clustered subjects (birds, frogs, flowers). They are the visual equivalent of a soundscape, by definition a compression of natural phenomena, archetypal and intense.

In 1933, Anderson married and settled in a house on his family's property. The Depression was under way, and he earned a living with WPA commissions and "widgets," whimsical figurines he and his younger brother James made and sold next to the Shearwater Pottery, founded five years earlier by their older brother Peter. But in 1937, Anderson, known to be moody, plunged into three years of mental illness marked by hospital stays (including two escapes) and disappearances. In 1940, he came home to his wife and children, establishing a solitary, eccentric way of life. By 1946, he had mostly departed the family home and divided his time between a little cottage by Shearwater Pottery and the offshore islands, especially Horn Island (although he took a few trips, notably to China and Costa Rica). He lived as a primitive on Horn Island; if it rained, he slept under his rowboat. But there, he produced a lifetime of drawings and paintings: waterfowl, sea life, birds, plants, trees, insects, and wide views of the islands and shore.

Anderson had an affinity for the dead and dying and occasionally captured an injured animal or insect, keeping it long enough to get it down on paper before releasing it back into the wild. In his 1959 log, he wrote about rescuing a wounded duck, a scaup, with which he slept. Each morning, before leaving camp in search of new plants and animals to paint, Anderson anchored "Simy" in the marsh to keep him safe. Over the next six days, he drew or painted Simy several times and tried to nurse him back to health. But at week's end, he returned from an expedition to discover his duck had died.

> When I went to take him in afterwards he was dead, with his head under water. I suppose he drowned trying to get away. I got very fond of him during the six days I had him. He made no pretense of liking me. I had to force food on him although he evidently liked the food when it was in his mouth. I buried him with a dead grebe on top of a sand dune by moonlight with the evening star just setting, and a French duck in the marsh saluted him.

Anderson kept daily logs at Horn Island from 1944 to 1965, when he was diagnosed with lung cancer. He died soon afterward, following surgery in New Orleans.

* * *

By 1988, Earl had grown restless again. "I could see myself doing the same things for the next twenty years, and that scared me," he said.

The new music scene in New Orleans had no real legs, he knew—I'd lamented the situation myself when I lived there. Even though I taught part-time at Loyola, giving me a little foothold in the music community, I found it difficult to recruit players and audiences for the contemporary works I cared about (Sandy Hinderlie's appearance later would begin to change that). Earl's uptown habitat was the same as mine: a trail connecting the Prytania Theater, Maple Street Bookstore, Uptown Books, and Audubon Park.

"Uptown was sealed in—nobody came in or out; I had no one to talk shop with," Earl says, capturing my own feeling of isolation in the late 1970s. Ellis Anderson, an artist and writer who lived in the French Quarter then, said she experienced the same closed world. "We joked that you had to have a passport to leave and reenter the Quarter," she said. "We stuck to our own little neighborhood."

· · ·

In spring 1989, Earl took a camping trip with friends to Big Bend National Park in Texas, and on a stop in Austin, he contacted Karl Korte, a composer on the University of Texas faculty who invited him to submit some scores and apply to the master's program there. A few weeks later, UT offered Earl a scholarship, and he went fishing for speckled trout on Grand Isle, a barrier island in Barataria Bay, to think it over. He remembers looking out over the water and feeling a certain, inner "yes."

"I hated to leave, but something told me it was in the cards—I got the scholarship—it was time to go," Earl said. "Even though New Orleans felt stifling, I'd never lived in a place where I had grown so attached to the people—they were so open and easy to talk to. My teacher at the dojo told me, 'We're always here if you want to come back.' When I left, I cried like a baby."

CHAPTER 6

Austin

At midnight on New Year's Eve, 1989, Earl and Vickie pulled into an apartment complex at Ben White and First Street, a busy corner in south Austin. Earl had rented a unit there, sight unseen, on the promise of trees, but the next morning he realized how big an architectural transition he'd have to make. "This place looked like a motel," he said. "The only redeeming feature was that the pool had an overview of Austin." Earl started work on a master's degree in composition, and Vickie found a job as a dental assistant. "Going to UT was, psychologically, like leaving a house with fifteen-foot ceilings for a cabin with eight-foot ceilings," Earl said. "I had entered a world where it's all about competition and ego, and here I was trying to carry with me a secret vessel of nothingness." He was referring to an essential precept in his Zen practice: *muso toku*, the attitude of no profit or gain for oneself—a parallel, perhaps, to the Atchafalaya's natural cycles and the plentitude that arises from within. Yet he didn't want to leave his thirst for intellectual expansion unresolved. He says he enjoyed researching and writing papers and discussing ideas with colleagues—a luxury that had often evaded him in Louisiana. "You enter a new town and you may not like it," he said, "but still, there's something there you want to fulfill."

Karl Korte, Earl's major professor, with whom he would work all the way through a Ph.D., remembered when Earl came to UT. "He'd already had a successful career in the printing business, and he wanted, in his midthirties, to get another degree in music. I thought that was a pretty gutsy thing to do.

"As a student, he was very curious, and we shared a great love of jazz, so we talked about that a lot. He would sit down at the piano and play passages from Miles Davis charts, stuff like that. He usually took my suggestions for his music very seriously, and though sometimes we would disagree, it was never anything but a pleasure to teach him."

Outside private lessons, Earl and Korte developed a friendship that continues today, though Korte, now retired, lives in upstate New York. "We would occasionally go out for a drink or two," Korte said, "and we talked about it all—man talk, but also, literature, philosophy, and so on. He's so well read. He was tremendously serious, much more so than I was used to, in students. And he's a tremendously likeable human being—I've always been very fond of him. He's an unusual guy. Very honest—no bullshit at all."

Hanns-Bertold Dietz, a musicology professor specializing in eighteenth-century music, agreed to serve on Earl's doctoral committee after Earl worked as his technical assistant for a multimedia course titled "Exploring the Fine Arts."

"It was while walking back from the College of Fine Arts Building, where I taught the class, to the Music Building, that we struck up conversations about historic, social, philosophic, or aesthetic topics related to art and music and life," Dietz remembered. "It was the breadth of his interest and the genuineness of his thoughts that made me agree to serve on his committee."

Dietz recalled that Earl, though an A student in his eighteenth-century music course, did not stand out in the class.

"When asked, he would always have thoughtful answers but would not volunteer questions, because—I later found out—he did not want to disrupt my plan and direction of presentation. He struck me as a typical Southern gentleman." Dietz later worked with Earl one-on-one in directed readings for his comprehensive exams, and vividly remembered "the 'calm' excitement" Earl brought to the sessions, especially concerning the question of the composer as moralist. Dietz also said Earl enjoyed teasing out the changes in Haydn's compositional process in his symphonic output between the 1770s (*Farewell* Symphony) and the 1790s (*London Symphonies*). He added that Earl seemed to him to be a procrastinator. "He had his own rhythm of work," he said. "He wouldn't fit into the typical corporate lifestyle."

Dietz and Earl still keep in touch. "All that trouble to finish the Ph.D. and he ends up where he is," Dietz said. "He chose to be with his mother; he felt obligated. But if he is unhappy about it, he doesn't express it. He has complained about the difficulty but has never whined about it."

* * *

Earl appreciated the "world-class ambience" at UT, which gave him the chance to solidify everything he'd learned on his own over the years. He reveled in music history, filling in the blanks between early and modern music, and learned that while composition teachers can coach and mentor students, "they can't teach you how to write." When he won a teaching assistantship, he began developing his own teaching abilities leading undergraduate music theory classes in sight-singing, keyboard skills, and melodic and harmonic dictation—in which one writes down, in musical notation, what one hears. He took in concerts by the many cutting-edge artists who passed through Austin then (the scene has since dialed back), among them performance artist Laurie Anderson; the Merce Cunningham Dance Company with electronic music composer David Tudor, who had succeeded John Cage as Cunningham's music director; and Sankai Juku, the Japanese Butoh dance troupe that came out of the 1960s Japanese avant-garde. One semester, pioneer electronic/multimedia composer Morton Subotnick was in residence at the College of Music, and Earl got to study with him. At the time, Earl was well along on a brass quintet and needed no more than a little guidance, so often he and Subotnick went out to eat Tex-Mex and talk about Subotnick's old days in New York, when he was first composing on a Moog synthesizer.

"I was in awe of him at first—I mean, everyone revered him for *Silver Apples of the Moon* [the first electronic work commissioned by a record company, Nonesuch]," Earl said, "and he had traveled the world. But he was just a regular guy. He told me about meeting Frank Zappa, who had a studio in a basement and had made oscillators out of car seat springs. Zappa was like a mad scientist.

"He also said, 'The first thing you do if you want to be a composer is live within your means—because the more you exceed it, the less time you'll have to devote to your ideas.'"

Subotnick had visited Austin for an electronic music festival a few years before, and I'd performed with him his *Passages of the Beast*, for clarinet and electronic ghost score (put simply, my instrument was hooked up to speakers and electronic controls Subotnick used to manipulate the pitch, timbre, volume, and location of everything I played, as I played it). Subotnick's music is penetratingly visceral and often concerned with the natural world and humans' place in it. In a program note, the composer wrote:

The title *Passages of the Beast* refers to the rites of passage, of beast-ness to humanness, the passion of the beast and human awareness joined. The clarinet is treated as both a very old instrument (through a series of invented fingerings to get some of the non-diatonic qualities back into the technique) and a modern instrument, paral-leling, more or less, the transition or passages from beast to human. The almost programmatic quality of the work is in keeping with the mainstream of my work for more than a decade. *Passages,* in particular, deals metaphorically with the evolution of the human spirit.

Earl also had access for the first time to willing and accomplished per-formers and the pressure to meet deadlines. That is, he had a professional structure that artists working in a vacuum lack and might wish for. And he had peers, among them a cadre of fellow doctoral students who called themselves the "Q Patrol," for their Friday night trips around Central Texas, hunting down the best barbecue. In the running were Mueller's in Taylor, the Salt Lick in Driftwood, the Elgin Meat Market, and Kreutz's in Lockhart. Kreutz's won out.

"The diversity of food in Austin added to my creative spirit," Earl told me, with a smile, though he doesn't deny his frequent trips back home for seafood. He had a south Austin Tex-Mex circuit mapped out, and a repertory of Asian eateries, too—all specializing in seafood. When he was studying for his written comprehensive exams, Eula, who was mostly clueless, at best bewildered by her son's exodus to Austin, sent him a check for one thousand dollars so he could go out to eat wherever he wanted. He chose one restaurant: Mezzaluna, an upscale Italian place in the warehouse district. "I spent eight hours a day prepping, then I'd go to Barton Springs to swim and lie around for two hours, and then to Mezzaluna for shrimp primavera. I did the same thing every day for two months."

Mark Wingate, a member of the Q Patrol and now a professor of composition and director of electroacoustic music at Florida State

University, recalled their common delight in a good meal. But he also remembered how Earl stood out from the other graduate students.

"What always struck me about Earl was the obvious love of where he'd come from. He was so steeped in that culture, so close to the earth, yet he was at an institution of higher learning. He had an intellectual capacity that was very impressive. He was quite erudite. He had a massive record collection and was a real scholar of composers like Takemitsu and Cage. He introduced me to a lot of music.

"The Atchafalaya informs a lot of who he is," Wingate continued. "You always knew it—he was always mentioning it. He was concerned about the basin and was disgusted with what the oil companies had done to it over the years. He lamented the constant assault on the land, the animals, waterfowl, fish, and oysters. I'm pretty environmentally conscious, but I didn't know about it until he told me."

Wingate said Earl regaled his friends with stories about Cajun cooking and Mardi Gras, and one year, they all drove down to New Orleans together for Fat Tuesday. Wingate described his friend as a natural storyteller. "He used vivid imagery I could never come close to imitating, but I remember one story about being in a boat after dark when the light was at such an angle on the inky water that he could see the eyes of an alligator. The way he told that story was so beautiful, so evocative of the place."

Wingate clearly recalled how Earl explained his time at UT: as something he had to do for himself, not a career move, as it was for the other graduate students.

"Nobody knew then that he would go back to Louisiana, but I just assumed it was a general possibility," Wingate said. "Louisiana defined who he was. He was hard-core.

"This sums it up: I'd go to his apartment in Austin, and you know how most people have the TV on in the background? Earl had his TV tuned to the weather satellite station—not the one with the beautifully coiffed meteorologists, but the satellite—that round thing that shows satellite data. Earl was a weather fanatic. Earl was unique."

When asked about the satellite station, Earl told me he used it as a timepiece while he composed. "It was a reminder of the earth's rotation, and the limited time we have on earth. It showed the way the earth looked moment to moment. No sound, just the earth. I found it very meditative."

*   *   *

In 1993, London-based electronic composer Stephen Montague and pianist Philip Mead visited UT and invited students to submit works for their upcoming tours. They selected Earl's *Silent Forests* for piano and live electronics—a narrative work depicting a forest's destruction, ending in silence. Montague remembers it as "a student piece," with its obvious ending, but it was effective enough to be toured. Over the next two years, Montague sent Earl postcards from several European cities, marking where they'd performed his piece. When a postcard arrived, Earl took himself out to dinner to celebrate.

By this time, the three themes that drove Earl creatively were clear: the perilous state of nature, the individual versus society, and death. His setting for soprano and piano of three Kenneth Patchen poems, which Earl titled *Diary of a Mad Poet,* mirrors this. The first and third poems, "All Is Safe . . ." and "Fall of the Evening Star," bespeak mostly comfort, not conflict. "All Is Safe . . ." pays homage to water as a restorative balm, with birds arising from it, ending thus:

> *Flow, water, blue water*
> *All is safe in thee*
> *Little birds*
> *The shadows of maidens*
> *O safe in thy singing*

But the central setting, "A Vision for the People of America," bristles with anger. "The slimy hypocrisy will end./You will go down in your filth," one couplet goes, and the thrice-repeated refrain strikes an ominous chord:

"The poets with death on their tongues/shall come to address you."

Besides the poems, Patchen was a natural draw for Earl as a pacifist and a jazz poet who had collaborated with John Cage and Charles Mingus. With hindsight, one can make another connection. Patchen was permanently disabled by a spinal injury suffered while repairing a car; Earl would encounter disability, too.

Earl's comments on the works he composed at UT reflect his aesthetic at the time and also point to the soundscapes he would one day assemble from the Atchafalaya's natural sounds. "The pieces evoked a presence and made a statement without regard to form, even though there was form, and without reference to technique, even though there was technique," he said. "In abstract expressionism, the canvas is a springboard for the feelings of the audience, so the statement is inside, and the artist translates it, or evokes it, on canvas. Feeling becomes form. In the *Heart Sûtra*, which we chanted in the dojo, form is void, void is form. That sort of sums it up."

Vickie Robertson says that in the later Austin years, 1993–1995, beginning around the time Steve Montague came to town, Earl started drinking more than usual and one night came home drunk, picked up a chair, and threw it at her. "Not so it would hit me, but to get my attention. Then I realized he was depressed. It hadn't dawned on me." The next day she got the number of a campus therapist and gave Earl an ultimatum: get some help, or else. Earl entered therapy. "He'd been through so much, with the guilt over his father's death," Vickie says.

Earl sees his troubles a little differently. "I was really flogging myself to get through the doctoral program. Two things happened: I started drinking, and I started going to strip clubs. Then all of a sudden, I'd find myself doing something ordinary, like sitting down in a restaurant, and just starting to cry, for no reason."

It got worse after the prolific composer, conductor, and author Gunther Schuller visited campus and, in a talk I also attended, told composers and other musicians that he got so much done because he slept no more than four hours a night—and the rest of us should be able to get by on that, too. (Somehow, we didn't immediately take in Schuller's haggard appearance and apparent lack of exercise.) To Earl, he said that it was a shame he lacked the opportunity to hear his pieces for large forces, like orchestra or wind ensemble. Earl says, "He was telling me that to fully develop as a composer, you have to experience the sounds you've made on a massive scale, and the only way to do that is by trial and error. But if you don't have the opportunity to work with those forces, what are you going to do? I got very depressed about getting out of school and looking forward to nothing."

Earl's therapist did his best to help but encountered a block. "You know zazen meditation," the therapist said to Earl, "so you have the tools to fix yourself. The question is, why don't you do zazen?"

Earl's answer: "I just felt that zazen would calm my mind to the point where I'd lose the conflict that creates the piece."

Earl cut back a little on the drinking and meditated some, but as he began work on his dissertation, a weather-inspired piece for wind ensemble called *Occluded Front*, he started smoking more—a habit he'd begun in New Orleans bars ("I bought them to go with beer"). It's the one vice of three he hasn't yet beaten, despite his serious bout with cancer. "I never had trouble quitting drinking," he says. "With cigarettes, well, I know pressure is no excuse, but with all I'm going through being a caretaker for Mom, I need something.

"For my dissertation, I bought cigarettes to help me concentrate. I'd be up at three, four in the morning, smoking and writing. My last semester, I did two real long pieces." Karl Korte told him, "Back off—you're having nervous problems," but Earl wrote more music then than he ever had.

Toward the end of his years in Austin, just before and after he finished his dissertation, Earl house-sat for my husband and me a few times. By then he was meditating more regularly; he always brought his zafu and meditated by the fireplace, and I imagined the living room felt calmer when we returned, as if Earl had realigned its molecules. But there was another connection I unconsciously made with Earl then, which a writer friend, whose daughter had died a sudden, untimely death, illuminated for me later. "We who have unexpectedly lost loved ones instinctively know each other, as you and I did," she said. "We recognize the kind of sorrow we share." When I think of this friend, and a handful of others, including Earl, I am sure she was right. My mother, the outdoorswoman, and my father, the man who would return to the farm, died together in a car accident on a marsh road a few miles from the Kennedy Space Center. I was a twenty-three-year-old graduate music student then, and over the years, discovering other members of my "tribe," such as Earl, I've realized the event defined me in ways I still struggle to clarify. In gathering together Earl's story, I've learned it's much easier to see the patterns in another person's life.

● ● ●

After completing his doctorate in spring 1995, Earl was invited, through a connection forged by UT, to spend a month in Sweden as a guest lecturer at Stockholm's Musikhogskola. While there, he presented his work and led discussions on American music. It was his first and only trip abroad, and he loved particularly the clean, light-suffused architecture and the availability of intimate, searching foreign films free of Hollywood bling and bluster. Once, he announced to an acquaintance that he planned to attend a Russian film festival. The friend advised him to skip it, because he'd encounter "nothing but bare landscapes and silence," and Earl told him, "That's exactly why I want to go."

Earl's time in Stockholm was successful enough that authorities there began planning an extension: a full year's residency, to be funded through the American embassy, probably by the Fulbright Scholar Program. But funds expected to be available were cut, and Earl returned to Austin, taking a job as an assistant at the university's Center for Teaching Effectiveness. He also applied for and received a three-week residency at the Atlantic Center for the Arts in New Smyrna Beach, Florida, to work with American composer Donald Erb, a contemporary of Morton Subotnick who combined live synthesizer and acoustic instruments, and sometimes included unconventional sound makers in his scores. I clearly recall playing in a performance of Erb's 1972 *The Purple-Roofed Ethical Suicide Parlor* for wind ensemble and electronic tape, which requires the woodwind players to set aside their instruments and blow on sixteen-ounce pop bottles filled with varied levels of water. The work evoked Kurt Vonnegut's short story "Welcome to the Monkey House," set in an overpopulated society where people are encouraged to solve crowding by checking into the parlor forever. Erb, though ensconced in academia for decades, was an *enfant terrible*—or an *eminence terrible*, as one of his colleagues put it. Once I visited his studio at the Cleveland Institute of Music and had a good laugh at his fourth-place plaque for the 1984 Kennedy Center Friedheim Award, to which he'd nailed a big rubber fish.

Earl and Erb took to one another, Erb appreciating Earl's talent, training, and conviction, and confirming that he was on the right path. ("He told me I didn't have to prove I can compose anymore.") He also advised Earl to write more music for small groups, a practical decision many composers come to. Electronic composers may keep live performers out of their work completely; one I know relishes the complete control it offers, with no need of rehearsal time.

Earl's residency at the Atlantic Center required he give a lecture and perform his solo piano piece *In Memoriam: John Cage*, written after Cage's death in 1991. He also volunteered his talent as a cook, one night making a giant catfish sauce piquante for about twenty-five composers, sculptors, and writers. "Everybody just cleaned up that pot," he said. But his most significant memory there had to do with Pad B in the Kennedy Space Center's Launch Complex 39, visible from Cape Canaveral Beach, as it had been from my hometown beach nearby, the silver rocket rising from Florida's coastal marsh. To Earl, it brought to mind the 1982 film *Koyaanisqatsi: Life out of Balance*, directed by Godfrey Reggio with music by Philip Glass and cinematography by Ron Fricke. In it, the artists juxtapose music with city and landscape images, conveying the message that modern life is crazy, out of control, and in desperate need of revision.

Koyaanisqatsi begins with a Fremont pictogram from Canyonlands National Park in Utah, followed by a close-up of the *Saturn V* rocket from the Apollo 12 mission. Earl remembered the cautionary Hopi prophecies Glass set for chorus. One sung phrase, translated, goes, "A container of ashes might one day be thrown from the sky, which could burn the land and boil the oceans." Robert Boissiere's translation in *Meditations with the Hopi* extends the thought: "But man has dropped from the sky the gourd full of ashes. It boils the sea, burns the land—it is indeed the mystery egg! It could trigger a rebirth or annihilate us all, depending on which way we go."

. . .

In 1996, Earl and Vickie Robertson decided to end their relationship but remain friends. Vickie moved to San Antonio to train as a dental hygienist, and Earl relocated to Houston, thinking he might join the Houston Composers Alliance and eventually find a position teaching in a community college. "You stand a much better chance when you get to know people and they know your music," he said, proof that he'd caught on to the way artistic communities in cities work. But he was obliged when he got there to take full-time jobs, first as an engineering assistant at Stone & Webster, then in the database library at Architects and Engineers, a reprographics firm, where he led a team scanning large blueprint drawings of navy cargo ships. The drawings were several feet long and covered every inch of a vessel—one ship could take three or four boxes of drawings. "They were delivered on pallets," Earl said, "and it would take a month or two to go through one pallet with six or seven people scanning around the clock."

Earl soon figured out that as a musician in Houston, giving private piano lessons, as he had done occasionally in Austin, would be more lucrative than teaching at a community college. But he wasn't interested in joining the local piano guild, where he might have gained some referrals. "I wasn't into the kid recitals, giving out little gold stars, and all that stuff," he says. Instead, in his free time, he began a private three-year composition project. *Remote Sensing,* the multimedia work inspired by weather patterns, was originally conceived in Austin and would require a full gallery installation—hardly the practical "small forces" piece Donald Erb had encouraged him to write. The project seemed to indicate not just Earl's willingness to persist as a composer outside academe's patronage but an inborn mission and propensity to create what he wanted under any circumstances. "An artist always feels the responsibility to reflect on the world," he says. By the time he began *Remote Sensing,* a task he describes as a "great catharsis" after jumping through so many academic hoops, he had stopped drinking entirely and regained a sense of himself as a creative individual working on his own terms.

Remote Sensing, which has never been completely and professionally installed, was Earl's response to viewing Launch Complex 39 from the Atlantic Center, overlaid with *Koyaanisqatsi.* One afternoon in the Nicholls State University Library, where *Remote Sensing* was stored until 2008, he spread out on a long conference table the more than 150 mounted data collages that dominate the piece and told me how the work came to be.

"When I got back to Austin from the Atlantic Center, I had a lot of time on my hands at my job at the Center for Teaching Effectiveness," he said. "I started reading about what was going on in the Arctic and the Antarctic—the thickness of the ice pack, weather patterns, the currents affecting the wind, the jet stream, the rise in sea level. I also took an interest in the Gaia hypothesis [that Earth is a self-regulating organism of interdependent life-forms and environmental systems], because there was a big debate about whether it was valid.

"After a while I used my lunch hours to search the libraries at UT and make copies of line drawings and maps and satellite photographs of Earth, and the satellites themselves. Also the ocean and the atmosphere, and especially Earth portioned out by latitude and longitude. And I had pictures of fish, whales, penguins, undersea exploration, data charts. It seemed amazing to me that with all this technology, man couldn't do anything to help or resolve environmental problems.

"Then I began making transparencies of the line drawings and other images I'd collected, and superimposed them on each other. Then I would take two transparencies, side by side, and turn them into an eleven by seventeen. They were composite images of composite images.

"I was just doing it to pass the time."

Also to pass the time, Earl began sampling underwater acoustic recordings—whales, dolphins, sonar frequencies—borrowed from a library at the Balcones Research Facility, where he worked a temp job at night. At this point, he was renting a room from a friend in Austin who had a home electronic studio—two tape decks and a sampler—where Earl could manipulate the samples, shaping and layering them. "I just sort of intuitively worked with the sounds to create a kind of a parallel to what the visuals would later be," he said. "I'd been influenced by Robert Rauschenberg and his collages and montages—that sort of thing. But this wasn't really a conscious project. One thing just eventually led to another. I had started something I never thought would realize itself."

A few months later, Earl lugged to Houston, along with his books, tapes, and records, two boxes overflowing with 11 × 17 composite image sheets. When he began work at Architects and Engineers, overseeing the navy blueprint scans, he got an idea. Why not dry-mount his images so they could be part of an installation?

Luckily for Earl, the head of the dry-mounting department was a friendly minister interested in his project. "I told him I'd never get a grant to do something like this," said Earl. The minister gave him permission to use the firm's dry-mounting facilities, and Earl learned the process himself, talking several pals in the department into helping him with what was obviously becoming a substantial project.

"It was a covert operation," Earl said. "A whole team working undercover for me. They thought it was kind of cool." The boards they used came from projects that had been returned to the company, and because they were different sizes, usually larger than 11 × 17, Earl and his friends had to enlarge the images to fit them. "I would leave things for the night crew, who would blow this stuff up and leave the photographs in a special place for me to dry-mount after hours. The owners didn't know anything about this."

One day, the minister said it was time to stop and move the project someplace else. It was taking up too much space.

"It was up to about 150 boards now," Earl said. "It covered almost the whole dark room. And I said to him, 'I wanted to talk to you about the possibility of lamination.' And he said, 'Now you're really talking some money.'"

Still sympathetic to Earl's cause, the minister signaled him to a room where large rolls of laminate, free samples from various companies, were stored.

"He brought out a couple of rolls of pretty hefty laminate, and asked, 'Will this work for you?' He charged me twenty-five dollars for it. So with a friend, I laminated all the boards in one night.

"I never really thought this would happen. I just ended up in a position where I saw a way I could get a project done. I walked out of A and E with a twenty thousand–dollar project and I paid twenty-five dollars for it."

By now, Earl envisioned an installation of boards and sound but felt it needed one more component: video. So he ordered footage from NASA's Goddard Space Flight Center and the National Oceanic and Atmospheric Administration. The videos of land and water, including flyovers of the poles, demonstrate how satellite telemetry, infrared technology, and different kinds of scanning are used to monitor the ocean. "It's what remote sensing's about," Earl said. "You know, man's ability to watch the change of the ocean and the atmosphere.

"The way I envisioned *Remote Sensing,* there would be two video monitors on opposite ends of a rectangular room, and the whole room would be filled with images of these line drawings and maps and fish and so forth, all in black and white, with low lighting. And the audio portion going on.

"Behind it all, I was pointing to a realization of man as just one of many agents in the universe. Some of the project references the Gaia principle, though it doesn't promote it. But all systems are interrelated. That's why I go back to Buddhism, which is a large part of what went into this observation. On the surface, I just intuitively placed and made these boards. In the same way, I worked with these audio aspects—I let my ear be my guide. But they were related and came together as a whole."

Besides awe, wonder, and the need to create something, Earl was driven in this project by the idea that "man is immersed in cyberspace— he has internalized the natural world and done nothing but quantify it." He refers to *The Disappearance of the Outside: A Manifesto for Escape*, the 1990 essay collection by the Romanian-born author and commentator Andrei Codrescu, a Distinguished Professor of English at LSU from 1984 to 2009. In the book, Codrescu condemns twentieth-century Western capitalist society, its thrall to images, and the resulting damage to the human spirit. In the title essay, he wrote:

> In the past ten years the Outside has greatly diminished in all its dimensions: geography, imagination, liberty. Transcendence has closed shop, or perhaps the last room in a shop that has been clos- ing since the Renaissance. But even simple escapes are no longer simple. One can no longer simply walk away anywhere but only into proscribed zones, wastelands between freeways, cul-de-sacs under floodlights. Even science fiction is distressed by our premature ar- rival into its territory: it has become nostalgia fiction, a gleam off the tail fins of Edsels and Sputniks. The unknown, once accessible in various ways, has been sealed off at the borders.

Standing among his data collages in the Nicholls State library room, Earl reflected on ways the disappearance of the outside can affect scientists: "Once you come to an understanding of something, you make a closed system, which freezes ideas in time. But variables change situations constantly, and so systems must remain constantly open. That's what disturbs them so much."

More and more, in Houston, Earl seemed to be living according to a reflection by Takemitsu: "Just as one cannot plan his life, neither can he plan music."

"I had the feeling that I had just arrived at the end of things," he told me. "Not just with jobs, but in the development of musical language. Music in the sixties had run through so much experimentation. The seventies were an eclectic time, and the eighties were a continuation of it. The nineties were a retrospective. We still have eclecticism, but you can only borrow so many languages to say so much. It seemed to me that the only place to go, in the arts, was to nature."

Of Earl's decision to remain outside the conventional patronage system (university positions, contests, conferences), his former teacher James Drew had this to say: "In Earl's case, the big postwar expansion of universities was over, and jobs weren't exactly plentiful. The scene was very political. Now, instead of what shall I write, it's how can I get a career, how can I be a celebrity? I think Earl was honest in a certain sense. Some people are ambitious in the world, and they're comfortable stepping out and letting people know about them. But some people just aren't cut out to do it, socially. I know about that myself. Some days I just don't feel like going out to that big to-do because I just don't enjoy it. And later I think, 'Well, I could have come out of that with a commission, or at least a connection of some sort.' There are people who network all the time, and I wonder how they have any time to write music, because they're always 'on.'"

Drew described just one tune musicians have danced to since 1945. Although the postwar years saw unprecedented growth in universities, they also brought new, technically advanced delivery systems for music. Wider dissemination of sound recordings and radio and television broadcasts threatened to sever the dynamic relationships between composers, performers, and audiences. Music wasn't necessarily shared "in-person" anymore, nor was it always shared with other listeners. The transistor radio with its little earpiece—the iPod's progenitor—offered private, insular hearings. At the same time, concert music succumbed to packaging and repackaging for a generic market, narrowing choices. Highly anticipated premieres gave way to the fiftieth recording of Beethoven's Fifth Symphony, greeted not with applause but a perfunctory review in a record guide. Once people could listen to the same performances over and over, their listening habits and expectations changed. Expertly engineered recordings dulled discriminating ears and led listeners to count on absolute perfection, even in live performances!

Increasingly, Earl embraced the Eastern concept of time, which he saw as an acre of land, in which birth and death occur simultaneously. "As in nature, there are many births and deaths at once. Sometimes there's confluence among them; other times they're out of phase." In Houston's busy heart, he took solace in regular visits to the Rothko Chapel, a nondenominational space whose walls are hung with paintings in shades of black by the abstract expressionist Mark Rothko. The opposite of traditional stained-glass windows that invite people to gaze out, the black paintings, lit only by an eye of natural light in the ceiling, invite them to look within. I know the chapel as well as Earl does, because during the same period he lived in Houston, I commuted there once a week for more graduate work, always arriving early to meditate at the Rothko before driving to the University of Houston campus. Our paths never crossed; I wasn't aware that Earl had moved to Houston. One might say that on that "acre" of two million people, we were out of phase.

Earl's ideas about time echo those of composers such as Glass and Takemitsu, who had a special affinity for water. In a short piece titled "Water," published in *Ongaku No Yohaku Kara* [*From the Margins of Music*], Takemitsu wrote of taking musical inspiration from Lake Tama, a reservoir that provides drinking water for Tokyo. It could have inspired Earl's developing musical response to the Atchafalaya.

> Thinking of musical form I think of liquid form. I wish for musical changes to be as gradual as tides.
> . . . I feel that water and sound are similar. The human mind conceives of water, a nonorganic substance, as if it were alive and

organic. And sound, which after all consists only of physical vibrations producing soundwaves (a secret code for language!), once heard arouses various emotions in us.

We know water only in its transitory forms—rain, a lake, a river, or the sea. Music is like a river or a sea. As many different currents create those oceans, so does music deepen our lives with constantly changing awareness.

While Earl was in Houston, his doctoral dissertation, *Occluded Front*, was premiered by the University of Northern Illinois Wind Ensemble and published by Ballerbach Music, a small company in San Antonio. Earl remembers that Donald Erb listened to a recording of *Occluded Front* and called to congratulate him and offer suggestions for revisions, which even the most accomplished composers will make after a first hearing. But neither Earl nor Ballerbach had resources to help the piece along, and *Occluded Front*, Earl's only published work, is now out of print.

CHAPTER 7

Return to the Basin

few months after Earl moved to Houston, Eula, now eighty, fell and broke her shoulder. Earl quit his engineering assistant's job at Stone & Webster, closed up his apartment, and went back to Berwick for two months to care for her. As soon as she could get by on her own, he returned to Houston and began working at the reprographics firm where he pulled *Remote Sensing* together after hours.

"That's when the lights started," Earl said.

Although no one knew it at the time,

Eula was beginning to suffer from Sundowner's syndrome, a manifesta-tion of dementia that brings on confusion after dark. For her, it took the form of seeing lights outside the house and sometimes spotting people she suspected of shining the lights on her. As her hallucinations increased, she began calling the Berwick police at all hours to investigate the ghosts.

"I kept getting messages from the local police chief on my answering machine," Earl said. "I talked with him about it some, and then one night, an old friend called and said, 'You gotta do something—get someone to sit with her, or move back here. She's really afraid to be alone.'"

Neither Earl nor Eula had any money to hire a caretaker, and no other relative stepped forward, so by July 1998, the solution seemed obvious. In a corner of his heart, Earl looked forward to leaving the city—it hadn't worked out the way he'd envisioned. But mostly, he was horrified by the prospect of living in Berwick, where jobs were scarce and a Cajun man with a doctorate in music was more exotic than an albino alligator. When the 2000 census results were released, his fears were confirmed. Just two-thirds of the adult population in St. Mary Parish (total 53,500) had completed high school. About 3,000 had earned a bachelor's degree, and only 836 held graduate degrees. The unemployment rate was close to 9 percent, and in 1999, some 20 percent of all parish families lived at poverty level.

"It was like—what am I going to do back there?" Earl said. "It kept me up many a night."

From Houston, Earl contacted school systems within an hour's drive of Berwick and says he received encouragement from a Terrebonne Parish personnel director in Houma.

"He told me, 'We're going to have a job for you—a new position in the gifted and talented program,' and I thought, that's great—I'll have my hand pick of the students, I can talk to them about music history and theory, and we can work on instruments . . ." A few weeks later, when he'd relocated to Berwick, Earl drove over to Houma to meet the man who promised him a contract would be "in the mail." Everyone knows how those promises usually turn out.

"That's to be expected down here," Earl says. "A lot of talk and nothing happens.

"This is one of the most unartistic places, anyway," he adds. "Athletics dominates the school system, and the coaches become the administrators, so there's a cycle in place. That and the oil industry are run like the military. There are a lot of good old boys. I remember what Clement Greenberg said of the abstract expressionists: 'These guys are really alone.' Well, I'll tell you about being isolated.

"I saw coming back to Berwick as the beginning of the end—or, more positively, the end of something, the beginning of something else."

Added to his disappointment in the local culture he'd once fled, Earl at forty-four, was, as his mother's caregiver, trying to make peace with living and composing in his old childhood bedroom, three feet across the hall from Eula's. In his first months back, Eula required a knee replacement and literally leaned on Earl for support and rehabilitation. She also required a psychiatric evaluation to confirm the dementia diagnosis.

"The doctor wouldn't talk to me about her unless she took that test," Earl said. "So we had to do it. She was so pissed at me afterward she hit me with her purse."

So began the last stage of Earl's relationship with his mother, which continues today, twelve years later.

Before, during, and after his struggle with cancer, he has shopped, cooked, and cleaned for Eula, driven her to her doctors and consulted with them, monitored her vital signs and medications, filled out insurance forms, and paid bills.

He sits with her during her favorite TV shows, takes her to the hairdresser's, and ferries her to dinner at her favorite restaurants in Houma and Franklin twice a week, "to get her out of the house a little bit." Occasionally a friend or relative drops by to visit and take a seat in the living room in front of the TV. Otherwise, Earl is Eula's sole company.

"The hard part is I don't have much time for myself," Earl says. "It's worse than cabin fever—it's an entombment."

It wasn't until late 2008, ten years after Earl's return to Berwick,

more than two years after his limited recovery from cancer and three years
on a waiting list for a state-sponsored home health-care provider, that
Earl and Eula received assistance in the form of a woman who spends
five days a week at the house, seven hours a day, cooking, cleaning, and
sitting with Eula (the hours were later reduced after state budget cuts).
"But neither I nor this assistant can do anything that will satisfy Mom,"
Earl says with frustration and sadness, and I know he's not exaggerating,
because I've seen Eula's own frustration expressed in pointed criticism—of
the woman's gumbo seasonings, her hair-combing skills, the volume on
the TV set—though she perks up for visitors and does her best to keep
up with conversations.

I asked Earl once if he'd ever considered making other arrange-
ments.

"The guilt I'd feel if I put her into a nursing home would be too
great," he said. "You can't take an old French lady out of her house, if
you can help it. Moving her would be like putting a lamb in a lion's den.
I won't do it to her."

He adds, "The *Heart Sûtra,* talks about compassion, and all along
I've had to remind myself of that. But at the same time, it's rough. I'll
just do it until I can't do it anymore. It's been a test of the compassion-
ate life."

* * *

At the beginning of 1999, six months after moving back to Berwick, Earl
found a job. It had nothing to do with music, books, or teaching—it didn't
even require that he be literate. But he needed something to do and was
told at his interview that he was "by far the most qualified" applicant for
the position. So he was hired as manager for Brownell Memorial Park,
a wildlife sanctuary and nondenominational retreat founded by an old
Louisiana family. The park lay a few miles north of Morgan City, across
Louisiana 71 from the East Atchafalaya Protection Levee, on Lake
Palourde, a lovely body of water he and Adam had often fished thirty-
five years before; it connects to Bayou Boeuf, where the old Thibodeaux

house stands. After Earl had been in the job a few weeks, he sent an e-mail to his Texas friends, who'd lost track of him after he left Austin. For all anyone knew, Earl had been abducted by aliens in 1996.

Earl's e-mail, tagged "I'm still alive," briefly explained his situation and new job. I replied, asking for more information on Brownell Park, as I was writing about travel for the *Austin American-Statesman* then and wanted an excuse to go to Louisiana. Earl explained that in addition to birds and a cypress swamp, Brownell Park was distinguished by a huge carillon he was teaching himself to play—in doing so, adding "music director" to his title. Later that spring, I drove over for a tour and filed a "postcard," a regular travel feature intended to convey an enchanted outsider's perspective. Here is an excerpt:

> *June 13, 1999*
>
> *Brownell Memorial Park, I discovered, is a 9.5-acre bayou refuge perfect for backroad idlers like me who prefer the surprises of indirect paths with no road signs and lots of greenery. The park is filled with thick patches of ferns, explosions of wildflowers, and graceful stands of moss-draped cypress that cast winged shadows onto Palourde's dark, undulating surface. Egrets, blue herons, and pelicans swoop in and out, and silent alligators ply the waters, their ridged eyes just visible above the gumbo. But what truly took my breath away in this quiet retreat was the inexplicable presence of a carillon tower, a 106-foot concrete column topped by a nest of bronze bells, rising up out of the swamp like a prophecy.*
>
> *The carillon, commissioned in the early 1970s by Claire Horatio Brownell, the park's benefactor, is one of the world's largest. Its sixty-one bells, ranging in weight from 18 to 4,730 pounds, were cast in Holland by Petit & Fritsen, the oldest bell foundry in Europe. When I asked Park Supervisor Earl Robicheaux about the carillon, he told me the magnificent bells have barely been played since the tower's construction and ring the hours only by way of an electronic impulse. It seems that the Brownell Foundation, which operates the park, has had problems funding carillon*

performances, and until recently has been unable to serve the carillon's natural destiny. When I lamented the waste of a world-class instrument, Robicheaux offered me a tour, and so inside and up we went, climbing spiraled steps to the tower's crown, where the clavier, or "keyboard" of the carillon, sits, its two ranks of wooden batons roughly corresponding to the keys on a piano. To see the bells, I had to wiggle up through a trapdoor in the clavier room's ceiling to open air, and it was well worth the vertigo to admire the bells and enjoy a breezy, commanding view of Lake Palourde.

Robicheaux's biggest task now is building financial support for renovating the moth-balled carillon so the park can offer public concerts. He envisions a series that includes visiting soloists, complementary instruments (such as a brass choir), and new, experimental pieces. The carillon, he feels, has the potential to become cultural manna, as enriching to the soul as crawfish to the belly or oil to the pocketbook.

"The carillon's importance lies in providing for an environment where man and nature interrelate," Robicheaux explained to me. "The carillon sound itself is nonobtrusive to its surroundings. I think of it as a gentle sonic beacon—a lighthouse of sound, if you will. Its resonances blend with the sounds of birds, frog choruses, the wind, and water. I think it shows how man and nature can coexist in subtle harmony, as opposed to man's alienation from nature, which seems so common now."

The Statesman's headline writer titled the piece "Standing Vigilant, Silently, over Sanctuary—Magnificent Carillon Hushed by Lack of Funds at Swampland Refuge" and in doing so, located the white lie contained within my piece. For the Brownell Foundation had not exactly encountered problems funding the carillon's restoration, but had turned a deaf ear to Earl's pleas to properly care for the instrument, and was unwilling to pay him for additional hours to prepare performances. The final disappointment came when the local priest who had agreed to work with Earl to produce a concert series was arrested for possession of child pornography.

I knew this story, but as a writer assigned a dreamy postcard, and Earl's friend, I had wanted to avoid sharp prose and protect Earl's job, while still offering an explanation as to why the carillon was allowed to deteriorate. Later, I realized I was mimicking a pattern already established by some paid spokespersons for the Atchafalaya: glorify the beauty, safeguard one's interests, and don't address difficult problems.

Eventually I found out how complex Earl's relationship to Brownell Park really was. In one clearing is a statue of a man in jeans, T-shirt, cap, and rubber boots, leaning on an upright log, feeding three raccoons. The man is the late C. R. "Doc" Brownell, nephew of the park's benefactor. In the early 1950s Brownell served in the Louisiana State House of Representatives and continued public service as Morgan City's mayor. He also happened to be the Robicheaux family doctor; he delivered Earl in 1954, and his nurse and wife, Pye, attended Eula and the baby. It was Pye Brownell, representing the Brownell Foundation, who refused Earl's request for remunerated carillon concerts.

. . .

Earl's new, remote positioning may have crippled his chances in the wider world, but it forced him to focus on the surroundings that had long fed him. Now, instead of making pilgrimages to other places, he spent the days in his own Walden Pond, listening to birds, discerning weather patterns, marking natural cycles, and waiting on the park headquarters' porch for occasional tourists. (Brownell Park is not considered a primary attraction. One popular guide to the region spent three times as many words on Morgan City's Mr. Charlie Oil Rig Tour.)

Although Earl knew familiar birds and their calls from his youth, he now had the opportunity to study them.

"I learned birding the old-fashioned way at Brownell," he said. "I spent all my time reading field guides, listening to calls, looking them up. Always, we had the white-eyed vireo, tufted titmouse, Carolina chickadee. And then it got to the point when I noticed certain birds, maybe even the very same birds, appeared in different seasons.

"Wilson's warblers would winter there; also the blue-winged warbler, and American redstart. Woodcocks and wood ducks among the trees—I learned right away how fast they could fly. And the wading birds in winter, especially white pelicans—several hundred at a time. They would fish along with four or five thousand double-crested cormorants, taking up one-third of the lake. One of the pelican's fishing techniques is to assemble in two lines, single file, and herd the fish in the middle. The cormorants took advantage of that. Several times, I saw a dozen bald eagles circling overhead, also fishing."

At winter's end, Earl observed the northern parula ("the first sign of spring") and yellow-rumped warblers, followed in a month by prothonotary warblers. During the spring high water, the park sometimes flooded, and Earl would patrol the path in hip boots, carrying a big stick to ward off snakes. "The yellow-crowned night herons came then," he said, "and I could walk among them."

In summer he observed the scarlet tanager and occasionally a red-eyed vireo or a yellow-billed cuckoo. At the end of the summer, "we got waves of yellow warblers. I think I set a record for seeing the most of those." After a while, Earl began posting to the LABIRD listserv and enjoyed the virtual community of birders reporting from all over the state. Early into his obsession, he reported sightings "that I knew later were wrong. Then I'd get a nasty e-mail from Jay Huner [an expert birder and retired director of the Crawfish Research Center at the University of Louisiana, Lafayette]. You know, once you hit 'send,' there's no taking it back. I always posted a correction." One mistake caused quite a stir on the bulletin board. "I said I'd just seen over one hundred golden-crowned kinglets," Earl said. "People wrote in to say it was impossible—no one had ever seen that many. They turned out to be ruby-crowned kinglets. The crown patches aren't visible unless the males are breeding—it's an easy mistake to make."

Soon after that, he got a close look at ruby-crowns on the park trail, when a flock of them walked right up to his feet, as if he were Saint Francis. "I didn't understand it," he says. "Maybe I was a heat source for them."

Earl also developed a relationship with a barred owl he named Henry. "He nested in the cypresses. We had a little game—I'd go down the trail and he'd fly ahead, perch, and watch me. Then he'd fly ahead again. I think he enjoyed it." Other regulars included a hermit thrush and a spotted sandpiper that sat on the same log every winter. Increasingly, Earl viewed the park as a collection of niches within a habitat.

He remembers one niche given over to eagles. "One day I was standing by the statue of Dr. Brownell and saw four eagles circling right over my head. One was a juvenile, and the others, adults, were looking at each other and making sounds. Suddenly, they all took off together, dove into the lake, and each came up with a fish." It was a no-fail fishing lesson for the juvenile, as Lake Palourde teems with shad and mullet.

Earl remarked on his growing annoyance with the carillon, which not only tolled the hours electronically but played sappy love songs he felt cheapened the park, and the birds in particular. He almost lost it one day on the walking trail, near an eagle nest.

"The adults were out fishing, and the juvenile was flying in circles, giving off distress calls," he said. "I could tell that some fish crows had raided the nest. When the adults got back, things really heated up—the eggs had probably been eaten. It must have been right on the hour, because at that moment, the tower played a lament—'Some Enchanted Evening,' or something like that."

"I hated that the carillon overromanticized nature with that cheap Broadway music. So I imagined one day burying a symbolic guy at the end of the trail—someone I'll call Mel, wearing a leisure suit and gold chains. He'd represent the record industry."

. . .

As 1999 wore on, with no change at home or in the park, Earl decided to take a night course with the Coast Guard to earn his captain's license. "I had this weird idea of giving bird tours in the delta," he said, adding that overhead costs quashed that plan. He was also tempted by an offer to captain a vessel out of Morgan City, but it came just as Eula was

scheduled for hip surgery. It seemed Earl would not easily shake the
stasis setting in.

"I started drinking again," he admitted. "It was the whole idea of being alone—why not? But then I realized that if I had a hangover, it could
be bad for Mom." Earl found a family therapy clinic in Lafayette that
billed on a sliding scale, and he worked with a therapist for six months.
"I had a lot of issues regarding abandonment and death," he said. "My
father—that was always there—and losing Kathy . . . everywhere I went
I had made friends, and lost them when I left. And now I was back in
a place where the world seemed to just stop. The therapist helped me
realize that letting go is part of life."

"But I remembered that my happiest times were in New Orleans,
with the Zen group, and Austin, where I had the sense of belonging to
a community. In Austin, you could talk shop." Earl wondered if he'd
ever be reunited with his intellectual and artistic tribe.

And then one day in spring 2000, a member of the tribe came
to him.

"I met Earl by sheer accident," Frédéric Allamel, a French anthropologist, explained to me during one of our conversations. "And it was
on a most unusual day."

Allamel had first come to Louisiana in 1987 to conduct fieldwork on
outsider artists in the southern United States. After a year he returned
to France, but in 1989 he came back to Louisiana and stayed four years,
researching the Houma—the only French-speaking Native Americans
in the United States—for his doctoral dissertation at the Sorbonne. The
Houma communities are scattered on islands within the delicate south-
eastern Louisiana coastal bayous and marshes—mostly those fingering
down toward Terrebonne Bay, east of Atchafalaya Bay—and Allamel
knew those settlements were in danger of washing away, like the rest of
the Louisiana coast.

Again Allamel returned to France, to complete the doctorate, but by
1995, he was once more in Louisiana. He and his wife stayed six years,
she teaching in a French immersion program, he continuing his research

on the Houma, publishing articles, and curating a tripartite exhibition of work by Houma bird carver Ivy Billiot, weaver and carver Cyril Billiot, and moss doll maker Marie Dean. Allamel and his wife made their home in Pierre Part, the French-speaking community north of Morgan City Earl had always been drawn to.

Frédéric met Earl after spending a day in New Orleans, conducting a private tour of his Houma Arts Triptych for the Duke of Orléans. The exhibit was mounted in the old U.S. Mint, a state museum in the French Quarter known as the Louisiana Historical Center at the Mint.

"That day had been a journey through time," Allamel said. "You know, this duke would be king, if France were not a republic. I met that man and his courtiers, and I would say they lived in a different century."

After bidding the Duke of Orléans and his entourage *au revoir*, Allamel started the drive back to Pierre Part.

"Usually I would go through Donaldsonville, and I don't know why that day I went through Morgan City. Then I passed Brownell Park, and I thought, well, I have always wanted to visit that park, and it might be the right time to do it."

Allamel turned around, drove into the park, looked around, and strode into the headquarters cabin, where Earl was finishing up a talk for a few visitors. Earl, intrigued by Allamel's accent, offered him a personal tour.

"He proposed to go to the very end of the park to spot some eagles that could be seen at that time of the year," Allamel remembered. "And while walking on that path, we talked about various subjects and realized we had almost parallel interests. We talked about contemporary music— Boulez, Luc Ferrari, Varèse. I saw his primary interest was in music, while mine was in visual art. My secondary interest in music was similar to his in visual art—you know what I mean. Both worlds. We also noted that we had some similar views on political issues and environmental ones, and when I left, we agreed that we would meet again."

The Allamels soon invited Earl to dinner, and for more than a year he was a regular guest in their home. Early on, Allamel asked Earl to collaborate with him on enhancing the Houma Arts Triptych, slated to tour the state. Specifically, Earl would produce an audio installation to stand also as an independent document chronicling the Houma language, which Frédéric warned, "might not be around twenty years from now."

The installation, *Voix des Marecages* (Voice of the Marsh), is based on a narrative storyboard in five sections: Houma Chronology, Ways of Living, Arts and Crafts, Prejudice and Persecution, and Land Loss. For materials, Earl and Frédéric collected oral histories from members of the Houma living on Isle de Jean Charles and Point Aux Chenes; they also attended Houma powwows in Grand Bois. Working as a team, Frédéric conducted interviews with artists and Houma leaders in French, and Earl recorded them. When the interviews were completed, Frédéric met Earl one night at Brownell Park to help him select from hours of tape the choicest moments for *Voix des Marecages*. Earl couldn't have done it by himself. He knew only snatches of south Louisiana French picked up from Adam, who had learned it at home but was punished at school for using it—a common practice in Adam's youth, effectively wiping it out in Earl's generation.

Then one week, because he lacked his own electronic studio, Earl left Eula at her cousin's house near New Orleans and continued two hundred miles east to a studio run by an old LSU friend, Dirk Billie, in Bon Secour, Alabama, to spend a week composing and editing the final composition. Although it is primarily a narrative sequence in a language few auditors would understand, the light, textured voices, nuanced south Louisiana French, and the quality of the recording itself set off a chain of soft visceral reactions, as if one is being whispered to or patted gently on the arm. The listener feels directly connected to the carvings, baskets and dolls, and the hands that scraped and sculpted, wove and knotted.

Within and between the narratives, Earl layered gentle night sounds—insects, barred owls, wind, and rain—all recorded at Four-Mile Bayou, his favored ground north of Morgan City. Occasionally in the distance, he introduced a low-level stream of powwow drumming and singing, as if recalled from memory.

The Houma exhibition, complete with *Voix des Marecages,* traveled to Nicholls State University, the Iberville Museum in Plaquemine, Southdown Plantation House museum in Houma, and finally, in 2002, the library at the University of Louisiana, Lafayette, where Earl took complete charge, because by then, Frédéric and his wife had moved to Indianapolis to teach. For the exhibit's opening, Earl presented a talk addressing Houma art, land loss in the Houma community, and the Houma's federal recognition crisis—for although it is recognized by the state, it was then and still is, in 2010, awaiting a response from the Bureau of Indian Affairs.

"When Frédéric introduced the world of the Houma to me, it raised my interest in land loss on the coast," Earl said. "All these people, living on floating land. Miss Marie, the doll maker, told me she'd moved five times because of the water. Baton Rouge [meaning the state government] doesn't have a clue. The attitude there is that the Houma are subhuman—when you start talking about lower Terrebonne, people roll their eyes.

"I think it's about class structure, the plantation mentality. They don't care about the elderly, either, as I found out. I turned out to be like my dad, trying to do the moral thing. I wanted to help."

In a two-year period, Earl and Frédéric had a full agenda. Earl wrote a radio play about the Houma, for possible dissemination to Houma children, and Frédéric translated it into French. "I also translated one of his environmental essays, the one where he compares oil rigs to insects sucking the blood of the earth," Frédéric said. Earl helped Frédéric with texts for English publications, among them a paper for *Southern Quarterly* titled "'Prophet' Royal Robertson's Architectural Odyssey: Psycho-Spatial Drama in Three Acts." Based on long interviews Frédéric had conducted with the outsider artist, the article captured Earl's fascination.

Robertson (1936–1997) would seem like a natural draw, since he was a local, living most of his adult life in Baldwin, working as a field hand and sign painter to support his wife, Adell, and their eleven children. But

after nineteen years of marriage, Adell left him for another man, taking
the children with her, and Robertson's mental health plummeted. He
retreated to a fantasy art world inhabited by colorful, eccentric aliens,
spaceships, futuristic buildings, and towering women, including the un-
faithful Adell. "Prophet" Robertson often clotted his pieces with scrawled
text: inflated proclamations, Bible verses, and diatribes against "wedlock
sinners." He even decorated calendars, assigning dates to Adell's
transgressions. His tools included paper and poster board, paints,
magic markers, colored pencils, ballpoint pens. With these, he filled
every available space in his house, and his paranoia spilled outdoors,
where he posted rotating signs warning "whores" and "bastards" to
keep out. In 1992, his home was demolished by Hurricane Andrew.
He died in 1997.

Earl didn't know much about outsider art, although Walter
Anderson, the Mississippi recluse he admired, possessed an outsider's
temperament. And Earl had encountered an outsider when, as a child,
he had fallen under the spell of a mentally disabled man named Julius,
the son of family friends, who lived in a shed behind his parents' house
and carved all day. When Adam and Eula called on the household, Earl
would trundle out to visit Julius. "He was one of the best carvers I've ever
seen," Earl said. "Julius could take a peach pit and carve out a monkey
sitting in a basket. With a pocketknife. He'd just toss it to me and start
on another one."

When confronted with Royal Robertson, then, Earl found something in the craziness to appreciate, and not surprisingly, a neighborhood connection.

"I thought, this guy's out of his mind," Earl said. "But I liked
the idea of writing going hand in hand with drawings. Royal's story
is very sad. I knew a woman in the area who talked about him as the
crazy old man who digs trenches at night. They wouldn't cash his
checks at the bank."

Frédéric also introduced Earl to the work of David Butler, another
self-taught artist, also from St. Mary Parish who, like Robertson, died

in 1997, but at age ninety-nine. Butler has been called an environmental art builder. His painted tin animals, human figures, and whirligigs were compared by one critic to the work of Matisse.

"Though I never met Butler, he was like a spirit to me," Earl said. "He made beautiful creations and was taken advantage of by the art world—he's the classic example of an artist who just wants to be left alone to do his work."

From Frédéric, Earl not only learned about self-taught artists who had lived and created in his own neighborhood for decades; he also came to realize that he himself was a kind of specimen discovered by the French anthropologist, although he's quick to say his friendship with Frédéric trumps any discomfort over that. His own "outsider artist" status dawned on him at the Allamel's parties, where he was, ironically, the only non-French speaker in a room full of teachers from the French immersion program.

"They would sit me at the head of the table, and then everyone would talk in French. I felt left out. I sensed snobbishness. If you trace the history of the Acadians, you know they left France because of the class system, so maybe part of that was still with me, and maybe I was just being oversensitive. But when I played my CDs for them, they liked them. The language of music doesn't have a nationality."

Confident in that knowledge, and boosted by his work and friendship with Frédéric, Earl saw his life in the basin begin to take on shape and meaning. "I felt I had come to the end of the impulse to compose, but Frédéric arrived and gave legitimacy to my work," Earl said. "And there was a cause behind it—the environment, and the people in it."

CHAPTER 8

Field Notes

When Earl created his soundscape for the Houma Arts Triptych, he joined a movement that had been around officially since 1993, when the World Forum for Acoustic Ecology originated. Describing itself as "an international association of affiliated organizations and individuals, who share a common concern with the state of the world's soundscapes," the World Forum states its members are interested "in the study of the social, cultural and ecological aspects of the sonic environment."

The group's leading light, Canadian

composer and environmentalist R. Murray Schafer, invented the term *soundscape,* meaning, in simplest terms, "the sounds that arise from a particular environment." In his seminal book *The Soundscape: Our Sonic Environment and the Tuning of the World,* Schafer named three broad categories within a soundscape: keynote sounds, sound signals, and soundmarks.

Keynote sounds function like the key of a musical composition, and in a nonmusical environment, they are the reference point from which all other sounds derive meaning. In the rural south Louisiana landscape, keynote sounds arise from geography and weather and include the whir and tinkle of Gulf breezes in cane fields and hardwood forests, the glissade of bayou waters, the squeak and patter of birds. Schafer wrote, "Many of these sounds may possess archetypal significance; that is, they may have imprinted themselves so deeply on the people hearing them that life without them would be sensed as a distinct impoverishment. They may even affect the behavior or lifestyle of a society."

Sound signals are "foreground sounds," or sounds people consciously listen to—for example, noon air horns, ambulance sirens, or, around the docks in Berwick and Morgan City, foghorns and railroad bells. A soundmark, or sonic landmark, is a sound unique to a community, and, Schafer argues, deserves to be protected. Brownell Tower's carillon counts as a soundmark.

Schafer and others have decried the death of the natural soundscape, engulfed by machinery since the Industrial Revolution. They recall the days when sonic cues, not visual ones, claimed our attention first, and believe we can still listen with as much sophistication as we see, if we will only turn our ears and minds in that direction.

Schafer didn't invent nature or nature-inspired recordings, however; such efforts had been going on for more than twenty years. For example, American bioacoustician Bernie Krause's 1970 album (with Paul Beaver) *In a Wild Sanctuary* employed nature sounds as background for pop-ish electronic pieces with titles like "Salute to the Vanishing Bald Eagle" and "Walking Green Algae Blues." Krause went on to become an important curator of natural soundscapes, capturing many in the field before development irreparably altered the environments he visited. To cite an example from my personal collection, his 2002 CD *Green Meadow Stream* preserves a fragile, chortling brook in the High Sierras. It took days for Krause to record enough suitable material and then create in the studio a natural, up-close sonic impression of that stream, as if the listener is sitting right on the bank with her toes in the water.

Houston-born composer and accordionist Pauline Oliveros, with whom I performed in Austin, has spent many of her nearly eighty years leading a related movement she calls Deep Listening. "It's a practice and a process," Oliveros explained to me a few years ago, over coffee in her mother's home in Houston. "It's listening below the surface to anything that's possible to hear."

In a concert setting, Deep Listening would comprise not just music, but, as with John Cage, coughs, dropped programs, and shuffling feet. It would also include performers' expressivity and listeners' responses—the silent communication connecting all present at a concert. When one is practicing Deep Listening, one is attentive to the foreground, the background, and the underground. It's another way to hear in layers, or on different sonic planes. It's also a nonjudgmental activity, springing from the Buddhist approach Cage embraced. Pauline has been a practicing Buddhist since the 1960s.

Pauline's fascination with sound began with her childhood in Houston during the 1930s and 1940s, before petrochemicals and pipelines turned a Gulf coast city of about 300,000 into one of 2,250,000. Back then, the local soundscape abounded with birds and insects and animals, just like Morgan City, 285 miles directly to the east.

"The sounds of nature were in the forefront," she said. "It was a very rich canopy of sound. I could listen for hours. Punctuating that were piano lessons my grandmother and my mother were giving in the house. My grandfather had a crystal radio, and I loved listening to the static and the crackle and pops. My father had a shortwave radio, and I was fascinated especially by the in-between sounds: the whistles and clicks. We had another radio on which we listened to network programs. I was fascinated with the sound effects on shows like *Fibber McGee and Molly*. Whenever Fibber McGee opened the hall closet, everything fell out of it. Each week there would be a slightly different configuration of crashing things. I loved listening to the way they fell—the rhythm of all of it."

For Pauline, as for Cage, as for followers like Earl, attention to all sounds eventually leads to a unified auditory experience, expanding one's perception of the world.

"It's like this," Pauline said. "You can't possibly take in all the details because our focal attention will take in about seven items at any one moment. But listening to the *field* of sound is different. You take it all in, but not as focal detail. Eventually it's possible to attend to everything by becoming as big as all you are listening to. You begin to experience it as unified."

When I asked her how she teaches people to listen so deeply, she said, "I begin by asking, 'What sounds remind you of home?'"

. . .

Earl knew of the Canadian movement toward acoustic ecology and Pauline Oliveros's ideas about Deep Listening, but he didn't imagine he was connected with either—yet. In 2001, after driving all the way to Alabama to finish the project with Frédéric, he thought about building his own studio, but mainly to compose electronic music. He might, he thought, use nature sounds in his work—purely, or sampled and manipulated like Legos of sound, or taffy. Then one day he realized, "There was plenty of material in Louisiana, and I was the only one recording it." In 2002, after hours consulting experts by phone, he acquired his used reel-to-reel Nagra for thirty-five hundred dollars from a CBS engineer unloading it to make room for new equipment. The Nagra is the Cadillac of field tape recorders; a new one would have cost seventeen thousand dollars.

"I was lucky. Right place, right time," Earl says. But for Earl, the price was still steep. He financed it all on credit cards.

So began his quest to document as many natural habitats as he could, in and around the basin. At forty-eight, isolated in his hometown, Earl had discovered his life's work.

· · ·

Outfitted with the Nagra, Earl began driving up to Lake Martin on early weekend mornings, intent on amassing a library of waterbirds, with an ear toward documenting entire soundscapes, or sound fields, not individual species. From Lake Martin, he branched out all over the basin. In his search for possible homes for his recordings, he combed the holdings at Cornell University's renowned Lab of Ornithology and noted only one bird listed under Louisiana. "The Louisiana water thrush—and it doesn't even live here—it's from South Carolina," he says.

Clearly, Cornell needed a man on the ground, and a collaboration began. The arrangement, like those with other volunteer contributors around the globe, was simple: Cornell provided tape, and Earl returned it, alive with birds. In time he produced a CD titled *The Sherburne Complex* and dedicated it to the near-legendary Baton Rouge–based ornithologist Ted Parker, who spent many years documenting birds in the Andes and the Amazon and contributed more than ten thousand recordings to Cornell.

Had I been in touch with Earl at the time, I would have appreciated the connection. Two years before, I had taught at Cornell and in early spring taken a birding course with a lab ornithologist. On Saturday mornings, we divided into groups and drove to the day's destination: a field, a forest, a farm. Once, we journeyed to the Montezuma National Wildlife Refuge near Seneca Falls, where transient Canada geese, mallards, and dozens of other waterfowl species clogged the marshes—a northern version of the abundance I had known in the South. All of us were encouraged to identify birds first by eye, then by ear, and I had trouble with that first step. How I envied the sharp-sighted engineering student who detected a female ruby-crowned kinglet flitting among the branches of an evergreen thicket. The female bears no red cap; she looks like any number of LBJs, or Little Brown Jobs. How could that young man possibly distinguish her, I wondered. She wasn't even singing.

During the time Earl began working with Cornell, liability insurance for Brownell Park increased, and the Brownell family decided to close the park. Earl was out of a job. He says it would have upset him more had he not grown weary, lobbying to restore the carillon. After his last day, Earl sent the Brownell family a letter, explaining the park's importance and thanking them for the opportunity to work there. He received no response. He went on unemployment then, certain that the only job he could enjoy in St. Mary Parish had vanished. But as word of his birding activities spread, he began to attract freelance work.

In 2003, Bill Fontenot, then director of the Acadiana Park Nature Station in Lafayette and longtime nature columnist for the *Lafayette Advertiser*, hired Earl with funds from the Louisiana Department of Natural Resources to help with a spring breeding-bird census in the basin. The survey couldn't possibly cover all of the more than one million acres; Fontenot divided the basin into six regions, and, as he put it, "We worked wherever and whenever and however we could. Most often we worked the habitats immediately adjacent to the basin's four hundred–mile levee system. I recruited top-notch field ornithologists only." Using a point count method, his birders set a time limit for places where they stopped walking to look, listen, and register species. "That gave us a birds-per-hour count, which is less rigorous than some, but we made do." Earl conducted his census entirely by ear, walking at a consistent pace, stopping at five-minute intervals to listen and count. To remember them, he graphed the calls in his mind like an electronic score.

Fontenot stressed the bird census's importance to documenting the basin's special character. "The breeding density for many woodland birds in the basin is off the charts compared to anywhere else," he said, "because the basin habitat holds a much more densely arrayed breeding situation." On a typical late spring day, a six-hour bird count on the twenty-mile stretch of Louisiana 975 from I-10 north to U.S. 190—the western boundary of the Sherburne Wildlife Management Area—might yield eighty detections of prothonotary warblers. "Divide eighty by six hours, and you get a number that can't be matched elsewhere."

Over time, Fontenot noticed how important the levee system was to bird diversity. "The expanse of short grass attracts a certain sweep of birds you wouldn't see in a swamp. It adds to the biomass of birds the basin supports. One question we still have is whether all the nestlings are actually surviving, because the birds are so jammed up. Is the basin providing an opportunity for nest predators? Is the Atchafalaya actually pumping out new birds? Is there a net gain?"

No one has yet studied basin bird survival, post-fledging. Regardless, Fontenot said, the basin's biomass is phenomenal. "There may be places in the Amazon Basin that equal this, but the decibel level of noise here is not common."

He added an appreciation for Earl's efforts, including and beyond the bird census. "We're both 'ear' birders—that's why we got along so well," he said. "And I don't know anyone else besides my wife [Lydia Daigle Fontentot, an advocate of wildlife rehabilitation and no-kill animal shelters] who is doing as much as he is. He's an amazing giver, an inspiration."

.   .   .

Earl continued developing his ear for an entire field of birds, enveloping everything from a red-bellied woodpecker marking territory five miles away, to an American redstart, whose thin, repeated *tsee-tsee-tsee-tsee* carries just a few hundred feet. It was important to grasp the whole habitat, he explained, because it was important to the birds. "Take one bird out of the group, and all the birds know it. It's like removing the bassoon from the orchestra—the musicians notice there's something missing."

And then came the installation for the Atchafalaya Welcome Center, providing funds to complete the home studio: computer, keyboard, synthesizer, and a Pearl microphone worthy of the Nagra. Lecture invitations from the Louisiana Wildlife Federation and the Louisiana Black Bear Festival followed. Except for a brief stint teaching music and art appreciation at a charter school in Glencoe, Earl had become his own boss.

                              * * *

In 2004, Earl got a call from Miriam Davey, a Baton Rouge naturalist who was developing *Louisiana Wild,* a pilot radio show for WRKF, the local National Public Radio affiliate. The show would highlight thirteen habitats over as many weeks. Miriam needed a sound man, and someone had suggested Earl.

"I wanted a radio adventure segment, like a National Geographic expedition," she told me one afternoon, as we watched birds peck seeds from her backyard feeders in central Baton Rouge. "Earl was willing to do anything and go anywhere. He was fearless."

The pair traveled all over the basin, but Miriam's favorite show zeroed in on southwest Louisiana's Cameron Parish—the coastal swath that Hurricane Rita would wash away in September 2005, a month after Katrina swamped New Orleans. The sparsely populated area, popular with migratory birds, offers several habitats: prairie, hardwood swamps, freshwater and saltwater marshes, cheniers, beach, and the sea itself. In mid- to late spring it often hosts fallouts, the phenomenon where thousands upon thousands of birds descend on a location, literally dropping out of the sky. The usual reason is fatigue. Typically, the birds have gathered en masse in South or Central America in the late afternoon and flown as many as eighteen hours across the Gulf all the cool night in order to conserve energy and avoid predators. They may have left on a tailwind, but if a north wind pushes down, the birds—some, like hummingbirds, weighing no more than an ounce—must expend extra energy fighting its force. When they reach land, they simply plummet, carpeting coastal Louisiana's fields, lawns, and porches. Especially exhausted birds have dropped to drilling platforms in the Gulf.

Miriam and Earl interviewed awestruck birders in the rain at the beach right after a fallout, and Earl recorded warblers and tropicals he'd never seen before—in so many colors, he said, they looked like Christmas ornaments. Against the surf, he captured a near-deafening mass of chattering and squawks and squeals.

In that show's second segment, Miriam and Earl sat in the Cameron cemetery, "listening to the sounds of the oil-installation beeps and squeaks and buzzers, and outdoor telephones, and birds." They boarded the Cameron ferry, a public craft that crosses the Calcasieu Ship Channel to Lake Charles. In the shadows of shrimp boats and oil rigs, the pair watched dolphins arc and gambol among the waves. The ferry's whistle dominated the sound field. Miriam pointed out the bridge shortage in south Louisiana. "No matter where you live in the region, you must regularly cross water," she said.

Other shows included a night in Belle River conducting frog counts with Jim Delahoussaye; a boat trip around Morgan City investigating the eagle population; an outing with a herpetologist in the Waddill Wildlife Refuge searching for reptiles, beetles, termites, lizards, and snakes; and a day in Sherburne, dedicated to the different bird habitats within the ecosystem there. One show even focused on birds and city traffic. "We set up in my backyard here at dark-thirty," Miriam said, "and started recording when the birds began to sing." A few peeps and cheeps here, a screech or squawk there, and gradually, the chorus jingled and rattled toward a joyful, swelling tent of song. By then, I-10, close by, had begun gearing up, first as a faint sonic seam, then escalating to the ubiquitous rumble we know as the bass line of city life.

Miriam said she couldn't have pulled off *Louisiana Wild* without Earl. In addition to his ears, his technical skills, and his willingness to heft bulky equipment through swamps and forests, Earl could captain a boat—essential for wilderness trips in south Louisiana.

"You know, he's a half percentist, meaning that he's typical of less than one percent of the population," Miriam said. "He's an undiscovered and underappreciated living treasure. He'll say he feels buried and rejected, but I think there's an element of choice for his obscurity and his private studio. The world doesn't know about it and is not likely to enter it. I think that gives him a certain freedom.

"He complains about Louisiana constantly, but he loves it, he needs it, and he can't be too far away from his muse: this land, this people, and this culture. He would literally be a fish out of water if he had to stay somewhere else for very long. He needs to be surrounded by people who live to cook and eat and drink beer and enjoy and love life. You know, people who don't do things in a straightforward manner."

Louisiana Wild was well received but lost its funding unexpectedly after the thirteen pilot shows. WRKF wanted to continue it, but Davey would have to secure a major underwriter for it, besides producing the series. "I realized the whole model was unsustainable the way I was doing it," she said. "I needed a staff of about twelve."

. . .

Earl was on to other projects. That year he independently composed and produced his first original CD, based on three years of fieldwork. *Atchafalaya Soundscapes* documents the basin's spring in three parts. *Dusk,* from the Lake Martin rookery, captures the merry riot of nesting birds: cattle egret, little blue heron, great blue heron, roseate spoonbill, common moorhens, and coots, occasionally sundered by the wing beats of roseate spoonbills flying directly over the microphone—wet blankets being shaken out to dry. Undergirding the frenzy is an alligator's mating call, the same one guests at the Atchafalaya Welcome Center now mistake for a lion's roar. Fittingly, a thunderstorm erupts, and as the rainfall thins out, *Evening* opens with a juvenile barred owl calling out to adults, heralding the organic swell of rhythmic nocturnal voices, high and low: green tree frogs, northern cricket frogs, narrow-mouthed toad, Gulf Coast toad, and bronze frogs. Overhead, owls hoot and sail. A "theater of the night," Earl calls it. *Dawn* guides the listener back to the Lake Martin rookery, with a spring chorus of indigo bunting, painted bunting, red-eyed vireo, prothonotary warbler, and Carolina chickadee. *Atchafalaya Soundscapes* is not the little brook and birdie track you fall asleep to on the massage table but an evocation of what it's like to kneel in a pirogue in a narrow lake or bayou, skin slick with sweat and dew, surrounded by the coos and burps and ratchetings of the living.

In his liner notes, Earl explained how composers and sound artists work with field recordings, monitoring the landscape, sampling it, reducing or compressing its time ratios, and in some cases reconstructing its dimensions within an altered temporal and territorial framework.

"The aesthetics of these various approaches to soundscapes and soundscape composition may ask us to question ourselves and define our parameters when making references to the real sound world," he wrote. "In a pure sense, the soundscape can be considered quite simply the total picture of an environment in sound. Within this larger sonic domain are regions in which one or more principal life-forms play a dominant role. The framework for capturing both territory and region is always dependent on seasonal variation, weather conditions, and the effects of sonic intrusion, or nonlocalized or mechanized sound sources in the environment. These latter effects have been widely discussed and debated for many years. Extreme cases of mechanized sound intrusion, or pollution, do play a significant role in altering the behavior of species. The problem is so vast that now, ongoing studies in the altered behavior of some species consider the role of mechanized sound components."

That would include studies of human beings, too.

Atchafalaya Soundscapes is dedicated to Adam Robicheaux's memory.

One day in October 2009, Earl and I made pilgrimages to two of his favorite bird- and frog-recording environments. We wouldn't take the Nagra this time because it needed repairs he couldn't afford, but he assured me we'd pick up a lot with our ears. When I drove up to the Robicheaux Street house, he was at the front door, ready to go, dressed in his usual hiking shoes, trail pants, and a denim work shirt worn over a faded LSU football T. I stepped inside to say hello to Eula, who was sitting with her walker at the kitchen table, watching TV with the latest health-care assistant. The first woman hadn't worked out, and neither had the second, third, fourth, and fifth. It wasn't all Eula's doing. One assistant was short term; another stole Earl's credit card number when he was away from the house.

"Where y'all going?" Eula asked us, and Earl answered, loud enough to cut through a game show's blare, "We're going to Cotton Road and Four-Mile Bayou, Mom."

"Well, when are y'all getting back?"

"We'll be back by five o'clock, Mom," Earl said, a little louder.

Eula sighed and looked down at the toiletry kit in her lap. The pleasant woman sitting with her was to help plump her hair that morning and fix lunch. Earl says Eula hasn't liked any assistant's cooking. "None of them can make a roux to suit her," he explained later. "Some can't even make a roux."

In the car, he volunteered, "I know it's a codependent relationship. She took the relationship she had with my father and moved it over to me. She wants me to sit with her every night to watch TV, and I can't stand the shows she chooses, so we argue about it. We finally agreed on one show: *Nancy Grace*. After that, I take my meds and fall asleep on the couch."

I said he deserved a posh spot in heaven for his devotion and asked if he's considered what he'll do when the inevitable happens.

"I don't know," he said. "I could stay here, because the house is paid for. But I might move to Lafayette—there's more going on up there."

           · · ·

On the way to our first destination, a black bear habitat south of U.S. 90 near Franklin, Earl offered some nature-recording basics. First, one needs the right equipment, primarily the Nagra and a sophisticated midsize microphone like Earl's, housing a single diaphragm and offering cardioid directivity—that is, it will pick up about 270 degrees all around. You also want twenty-five feet of line with which to send the mike into the sound field. Then you need to know the species call and from where it is calling.

"Say, you're in the woods, and over here you hear a tanager, over here a bunting, and over there a yellow-breasted chat. Well, the bunting and the chat are going to be calling almost all of the time. The tanager will call, but intermittently. So I'd place my microphone in a spot that would pick up the bunting and the chat straight on with the cardioid and capture the tanager from the side."

Earl especially likes to record birds around water, because they often congregate in the vicinity to eat, or perch on lower branches of trees and bushes to drink. Here, he can easily capture birds' three basic utterances: calls ("I'm here"), chip notes ("I'm right here"), and songs. And the rush and gurgle of water make a good background. They cover up unwanted sounds, Earl says, and "a little splash is wonderful.

"Now, frogs call in groups," he continued. "There's the impression that they're all over the place, but they're not. You may have a group of six here, and maybe eight over there, and what they're doing besides calling for mates is defending themselves from predators. Specifically, they mean to confuse the owls—the only real predators frogs have in the basin, besides snakes. And owls have directional hearing. One side hears the highs, the other hears the lows, and they gather it in, like a dish. The owl, turning his head 360 degrees, tries to find out where this frog sound is coming from, and when a full chorus is going on, he has a very hard time."

When gathering a soundscape, Earl doesn't just juice up the Nagra in one spot and kick back all day. He's walking and riding about, hunting for different localized sounds. Sometimes he sets the Nagra and mike on his car hood or on the ground; other times, especially with migratory songbirds, like the northern parula and the cerulean warbler, which stay high in the trees, he'll use a tripod and a boom.

"They're kind of faint, but I can zoom in on them," he says. The closer he can get to anything, the better, because there are no reflective surfaces outdoors, as in a concert hall. "You have to listen carefully to the foreground, middle, and background. Sometimes what you think is not dynamic turns out to be dominant in the studio. So it's important to consider register and sound source alike when recording—you have to listen with the mind of the studio itself.

"In summer I might find an area of cricket frogs, set my mike on the car hood for a little while, and capture that sound field. (In the winter you can't do that, by the way, because the mike will pick up the sound of the engine cooling off. You've got to use a stand.) Then I'll go down the road, find another set of frogs, capture that sound field. Maybe there's an area of Gulf Coast toads calling over here, and I'll capture that. The trick is to tiptoe around other sounds, like planes and boats and gas wells. With those in the picture, it's possible to leave the mike on all day and get almost nothing you can use."

Earl cites night outings when he thought he had the perfect conditions for recording frogs, until a tugboat a good five miles away chugged into the sound field, and he had to shut down the recorder for two hours until it passed. And if another tugboat bellowed, Earl would pack up and go home. "I'm not going be bit up by mosquitoes that long," he said. Even a passing car can cause problems with birds. Some may still call, but it will take an hour for the full chorus to return to its original, unbridled density.

• • •

Turning south off U.S. 90, we crossed railroad tracks to Cotton Road, a short, wooded byway that leads to an outlet from the Atchafalaya main channel. Very soon on our right, the trees parted for the entrance to the Atchafalaya Golf Course at Idlewild—according to *Golfweek Magazine*, the "#1 Best Course You Can Play in Louisiana in 2008 and 2009." I swerved in to see it, and Earl humored me, but he wouldn't get out of the car. The 175-acre public golf course, he said, was carved from critical habitat for the Louisiana black bear, listed as a threatened species under the Endangered Species Act back in 1992.

"Can you believe it?" Earl said, in the same tone he used on a previous trip, when we'd encountered the decked-out slave cabin. "Who would put a golf course in the middle of this?"

I'm no golfer, but I could see what might attract them: long, groomed open spaces, where once, dense bottomland forest sheltered wildlife. However, Earl hadn't remembered this tract was a dairy farm before it became a golf course, and thousands of wooded, undisturbed acres have always surrounded it. Of that generous habitat, Earl's disability attorney

Scott Ramsey co-owns or holds substantial interests in about nine thousand acres, and he and his partners have pledged to keep as much of it undisturbed "as long as we possibly can—at least through our lifetimes, as long as the surrounding areas are not developed," Ramsey told me. Part of his property includes a hunting club, a reminder of the positive role these clubs play in preserving Louisiana's hardwood forests. In fact, Ramsey's property has recently become a focal point in the search for the mythical ivory-billed woodpecker. In a 2004 chance meeting with Jay Huner, Ramsey, who was not familiar with the various species, learned that ivory-bills were alleged to nest in the area and told Huner he believed he had seen the birds on his land. The Louisiana Nature Conservancy commenced a search there in 2005 but was interrupted in August by Hurricane Katrina. Though property damage was light, the storm might have sent birds farther north into the basin. As if that weren't enough, a helicopter crashed on Ramsey's land the following March and set fire to parts of the search site. The Nature Conservancy's ivory-bill quest came to a halt then, but both Huner and Ramsey believe they have spotted ivory-bills since. At this writing, another search is taking place, though Ramsey is not at liberty to say who is conducting it. He feels certain that eventually, the ivory-bill will be documented in the area.

Along with the possible ivory-bills, Ramsey's acreage supports a black bear population, which makes sense, since both birds and bears love the grubs propagating in rotting trees. The bears, born of a remnant that survived hunting and trapping by hiding in hollow trees lumbermen spared, are, it seems, taking over. According to biologist Paul Davidson, executive director of the Black Bear Conservation Coalition in Baton Rouge, a critical mass of breeding-age females led to a population explosion that began ten years ago. The bears famously lurk around the golf course and its wetlands and have begun to cross U.S. 90, formerly their northern boundary, to root around residential neighborhoods. Recently, says Davidson, special funding bought nine hundred bear-proof garbage containers for citizens and paid for a supervisor to work with the community and the waste disposal company.

Scott Ramsey is concerned about the bear problem. "The sows are now producing mostly three cubs, not two," he said. "On a trip around the property, it's not unusual to see fifteen or sixteen bears—an unbelievable sight." He added that so far, the bears are more nuisance than threat, but he worries that children trespassing in the area ("and they do—I would have, when I was a kid") will set foot there at the wrong time. "At some point, a bear, just like a person, is going to have a bad day," he said.

The bears are quite comfortable around people. Ramsey cited the recent experience of a friend who killed a two hundred–pound feral hog on the property and posed his gun on the animal long enough to take a picture with his phone camera. As soon as the man started climbing back into his hunting stand, a large bear lumbered in like a late-coming guest and made off with the hog. Not to be cheated of his prize, the hunter dropped to the ground and was "off in hot pursuit" until the bear finally dropped it.

. . .

Back on the road, with its rustling trees, flowering weeds, and whirling grasses, I thought about how many common roads I'd driven during my life, and how expendable they'd seemed. Tangle of this, topping of that— to the person interested in moving quickly from A to B, or worse, Z, the scenery could be a nuisance, an affliction on the eyes, where novelty was wanted. Though some people don't care about movement. Earl told me once about a cousin who drove up to the old Thibodeaux place on Bayou Boeuf in a brand-new Cadillac, eager to show off the sleek, finned auto to the old people. "Just where do you need to go in that thing?" Aunt Ida, the perpetual mourner, asked, and wafted back into the house.

Where is it we need to go? Where do *I* need to go? In my travels, I sometimes feel I'm in a rush to a destination as phantom filled as the Atchafalaya Basin. "There is no there there," Gertrude Stein famously wrote of Oakland, California, when she returned to visit her childhood home and couldn't find it. And I think, there used to be a there for me in Florida, but it's all over. Family gone, Space Program ditched, town slumbering under a cloak of abandonment. I still return to check on the protected length of beach and wildlife and eat at a classmate's popular seafood restaurant. But my family and the culture I knew, a weird blend of rednecks and rocket scientists, have departed.

Earl interrupted my reverie. "Black willow, sugar maple, water locust, cottonwood, cypress, sycamore, pine," he was saying. "A real diverse habitat, but it's important to note what attracts birds: Virginia creeper, trumpet vine."

I slowed down and stopped the car by a field. "Here's an area that painted buntings love," Earl said, "especially in ragweed season. The height of allergy season, when you're almost dead. They come out in the road and take dust baths—find the densest ragweed they can find and roll around. They're beautiful birds, but I'm telling you, you pay for it."

We got out and walked a way into the field, listening. Mockingbird, Carolina wren. The October sun bore down on us quickly; the temperature stalled around eighty, intermittently cooled by a scarf of breeze. I bent down to examine a square foot of field beneath my feet and saw five kinds of growing things budging and bursting and spiking up from the soil, four shades of green, one of yellow, leaves like coins and spears and hearts, curling into and around one another, scrambled and tumbled, wholly art.

Earl stood silent for another few minutes, listening. Then he said, "I've recorded birds here more than thirty times."

"Why this one, out of so many roads?" I asked.

"My dad and 1 used to come down it a lot when I was a kid," he said. "Just to ride."

. . .

We drove down to the junction where the road meets a borrow pit running parallel to the outlet channel and stepped out again, waving to an Army Corps employee leaving the channel levee in a truck. Here was a different habitat: lots of cane, attractive to yellow-throated warblers and indigo bunting. Earl has recorded eastern towhee, blackbirds, marsh wrens, Carolina wrens, tanagers, and various waterbirds here, too. "Migratory birds have used this route for generations," he said.

I suggested the borrow pit might be a good place to canoe or kayak.

"Maybe so," Earl said. "Once in a while I come across an alligator here, but I've never seen one turn over a kayak."

If we could walk slightly southwest from here in a straight line, we'd wind up stuck in the mudflats between the two young deltas: Wax Lake and Atchafalaya. A few human lifetimes from now the deltas will meet, two spreading fronds of silt lying shoulder to shoulder, and there, another habitat will spring from the gel of new earth.

Earl and I looked out toward the Gulf. "How do you capture a sound out here?" I asked.

"Crawling for a thousand yards in the mud," he said. "But I love it. I mean, I absolutely love it."

Now we were headed north toward Four-Mile Bayou, on the basin's east side, about twenty miles past Brownell Park. Munching the apples I'd brought, we drove along the levee road through narrow spreads of double-wides and cottages, each nameless hamlet possessing a seafood or barbecue shack and a home-based service like saw sharpening or hair styling. Finally, Louisiana 70 veered east, away from the levee. The hamlets dwindled down to a trailer here, a plywood church there. Earl pointed to a turn off the main road, and we plunged into a cathedral of trees, of rare second-growth cypress. The caliche road barely supported us; water met the tires on either side. I rolled down the windows and heard only natural sounds: birds, a few daytime frogs, and trees swishing gently in the breeze.

"This might be it," said Earl. He paused. "No, this is not it."

"Where is it?" I asked.

"It's the next one."

I didn't know what my friend meant by "the next one."

The next curve? The next wide place in the road? I scanned the streams and marsh cupping our slender path. White herons, great blues, a duck that rocked over like a pushed toy before I could name it.

"Slow down here," Earl said.

The car was practically idling.

"Right in there," he said.

I stopped. To the right, the water widened just a little, giving into a treed thicket of mixed grasses and buttonbush.

"It's my favorite spot in the whole basin," Earl said, and now I knew it, even in daylight. It was the place he'd taken me years ago in the middle of the night to hear the rain-forest philharmonic.

CHAPTER 9

Cancer and Katrina

fter he completed *Atchafalaya Soundscapes* in 2004, Earl made a few attempts to sell it in St. Mary Parish—in a Cuban restaurant, a framing shop, and the Yellow Bowl. But he had no instinct for marketing nor the wish to develop one. "I decided it was pointless to drive around, picking up twenty or thirty bucks at each place, keeping track of it," he told me. "I can't even remember where I was selling them. There could still be some out there." I vouched for that—I'd seen them at the Acadian Cultural Center gift shop in Lafayette.

What would Earl do with the one thousand CDs he'd produced, paid for, and stacked in his bedroom closet? Leave them for someone to discover later? He finally came up with a better solution: donate them to Atchafalaya basinkeeper Dean Wilson, to sell or use to benefit the organization's conservation efforts. Later, he would give Basinkeepers the copyrights to two more soundscape CDs, *Sherburne Soundfields* and *Maritime Atmospheres*. "It's the best way I can contribute to the basin," he said.

In 2005, he created *Natural Abundance,* an audio installation for the new Louisiana State Museum in Baton Rouge, working with a Boston media company the museum had hired. At first, the company only wanted Earl to gather nature recordings that its own engineers would use as raw material. He told me how it went, dealing with corporate managers sixteen hundred miles away.

"The company sent me these e-mails saying they wanted to 'cast a wide net' to get all the birds. Go to this library, go to that library, they said. I told them, look, the recordings are going to have different compression ratios, so the backgrounds will be different. And what will you do when you start to combine birds, and you don't even know what birds are here? Are you going to use a bird that lives in the Antarctic or something? I've got all these things set up in my archive now!"

Earl overnighted a copy of *Atchafalaya Soundscapes* to Boston, and a manager called him the next day, asking how much he'd charge to produce a five-minute installation representing four seasons in Louisiana. Earl balked. "I told them nature takes more time than that," he said. Eventually they settled on about eight minutes. *Natural Abundance* is part of a permanent south Louisiana history exhibit on the museum's first floor.

Earl finished the recording before deadline, as he had also received a Peace and Justice Initiative Grant from the Methodist Board of Church and Society to collect oral histories along Louisiana's endangered coast-line. He would edit the voices for an installation to accompany *Vanishing Wetlands,* a traveling exhibition on Louisiana's coastal land loss and part of *Marsh Mission,* an ongoing project by photographer C. C. Lockwood and painter Rhea Gary. Earl would also work with videographer Bennet Rhodes on *Losing Louisiana,* an oral history DVD to be screened at the exhibition. As well, it would exist as an independent document on coastal land loss.

Most individuals Earl spoke with for these projects lived in Point Aux Chenes and Isle de Jean Charles, two villages he'd become acquainted with when he worked on *Voix des Marecages* with Frédéric. Isle de Jean Charles is an old Houma community bobbing at the end of a road that each year loses a few more feet of oaks and asphalt to the sea. Earl's raw recordings represent a handful of old families like the Naquins and Dardars and Billiots who have occupied the coast for generations—and as such, represent a significant contribution to Louisiana's oral history.

· · ·

By April, Earl had finished the *Vanishing Wetlands* project and begun working with John Amrhein, a Berlin-based photographer who had, like Frédéric, happened to stop by Brownell Park one day and found Earl sighting birds from the ranger cabin's porch swing. The two had a connection: John's grandfather had owned a diesel dock on the Atchafalaya and patronized Adam's barber shop when Earl worked there shining shoes.

John's Louisiana roots stretch back to the 1780s in Terrebonne Parish, snug next to St. Mary. His mixed heritage—French, German, English, German Jewish, Scots-Irish, Maltese, Italian, and Irish—is all American. "My nineteenth-century ancestors here included farmers, plantation and slave owners, and at least one lawyer/politician," John told me. "Rich and poor. Louisiana is more of a melting pot than you'd think. I don't have a clear heritage like Earl's." Born in Baton Rouge, John grew up in Houston.

"But we still ate gumbo, chicken stew, and had a freezer full of stuffed crabs and other seafood brought back from Louisiana." John guesses he flies back to Louisiana a lot because living in Berlin has brought out his "American-ness." Maybe he's a little homesick.

Together, John and Earl dreamed up *Voices of the Atchafalaya*, a photo exhibition showcasing longtime residents in the basin and backed by a soundscape: nature sounds and oral testimonies by the subjects speaking about their connections to nature. The pair interviewed and photographed more than a dozen individuals, capturing stories and voices as musical as the birds and water and foghorns that accompany them.

"Earl had a pretty clear vision of what he wanted from the project, and that vision directed much of it," John said. "He focused the project on particular themes, and afterward, I chose what was appropriate from the photographs I'd taken. Twice, he suggested we bring people who had worked as shrimpers to the river in Morgan City and photograph them in front of the shrimp boats. Another night, we took a ride out toward Belle River, and at a boat landing I got a shot of a man about to go frogging, and another picture of a drawbridge operator."

John added, "Multimedia projects have become very common with photographers, but I haven't seen one with a full-fledged sound component. Most are simpler recordings from interviews, with some ambient sound, overlaid with photographs. Usually it's all done by one person, but I think such projects call for at least two people."

In July 2005, Earl completed his portion of *Atchafalaya Voices*, a CD that ran over an hour. It was his third major project in six months. He and John had no funding for their show—they created it because they wanted to. Later, when the installation was unveiled at the Louisiana State Museum–Patterson, they each received five hundred dollars.

▪ ▪ ▪

I didn't know anything about Earl's soundscape work, then. A few months after I wrote about the Brownell Park carillon, my marriage dissolved, and I left Austin for Cornell, then moved to Laramie, Wyoming, to teach at the state university. Consumed with inventing a new life in the Rocky Mountains, I lost touch with several friends, including Earl. I was on another planet now, slinging my weight across the Snowy Range in summer, slogging along the Vedauwoo formations' trails in winter,

snow-shoed and chap-faced. I loved it. Yet in time, I grew homesick for
the South, and by my fourth year, I was running down to Austin or New
Orleans for every major holiday and many minor ones, too.

In 2005 I found a job in North Texas, and on an early June day moved
down, leaving eight inches of fresh snow behind me. A few weeks before,
at a farewell concert, a percussionist friend and I had premiered a piece
we had composed for narrator and percussion, with a text based on my
experiences listening in the Atchafalaya with Earl. This text, evoking
a warm evening of bird and insect calls, had languished in a notebook
for more than a year—I had written it to entertain myself one subzero
weekend. Now, as I drove the I-25 corridor south through Colorado and
turned east into the Texas Panhandle, I grew determined to visit Louisiana as soon as I got settled. I have to get back down there, I thought.
I have to listen in the basin again and see Earl, if he's still there.

But before I could plan such a trip, Hurricane Katrina wasted New
Orleans on August 29, and like everyone else with a friend or relative
who might have been in the storm's path, I tapped into all the media
outlets like a crazy person, praying for good news. I assumed that by now,
Eula had died, and Earl had perhaps moved to New Orleans. Where
would he choose to live? In a double shotgun on Magazine Street, near
the galleries and coffee shops? In a funky row house in the Faubourg
Marigny? A midcity bungalow? No matter where he had wound up, he
was lost to me, so I registered my missing person on the American Red
Cross Web site, logging on every hour or so for new information. I saw
one Earl Robicheaux listed there, but he was last known to be in Charity Hospital undergoing chemotherapy. I was sure "my" Earl was alive
and well.

And then one day somebody posted a new inquiry for the Charity
Hospital Earl Robicheaux and supplied a middle initial, C, which is also
"my" Earl's, and my stomach seized up. I e-mailed this person and asked
if she was looking for Earl, the musician.

"It's the same one," she replied.

"May I call you?" I asked.

Natha Booth, a biologist who was married at the time to Basinkeeper Dean Wilson, told me what had happened to Earl. In May, he had been diagnosed with Burkitt's lymphoma, a rare cancer lodged in the intestines, and usually developed by children in equatorial Africa. Earl had just turned fifty. Because he lacked health insurance, he had been admitted to the Charity system in August and had just begun radical chemotherapy treatments when Katrina hit.

"We love Earl," Natha said. "And we're concerned—it's been four days, and they still haven't evacuated Charity."

"I'll find him," I said.

After Natha and I hung up, I learned Charity had just been evacuated. Many New Orleanians had been taken to Houston, so I called a friend there.

"See anything in the papers?" I asked. "A list of names?"

No, she had not, and how did I expect to find anyone down there? She had just returned from the Brown Convention Center, where the clothing she donated was instantly snatched up.

"There are thousands and thousands of evacuees," she said. "You should probably forget about it." But an hour later, she called back. "There's an article in the *Houston Chronicle* about Katrina survivors. They quote a man named Earl Robicheaux."

It would be just like Earl, I thought, to volunteer extended commentary on the situation, given the chance.

I found the article online, then e-mailed the reporter expressing my concern, and Natha's. Was he the right Earl Robicheaux? Indeed, he was our Earl Robicheaux—he was lots of people's Earl Robicheaux. It turned out the reporter was a friend of Earl's former partner Vickie Robertson. Vickie, who knew Eula was still alive and that Earl still lived with her, had found him first and given the reporter their home phone number. "He sure has the women looking for him," the reporter said.

I asked the reporter for Vickie's number and dialed it. Vickie said Earl had been taken to Baton Rouge General for assessment and was now at home, resting from the ordeal—although he had not been too exhausted to refuse a phone interview with the *Chronicle* from his hospital bed. Soon he would return to Baton Rouge General to resume treatment under a new doctor. "He'll be so glad to hear from you," Vickie said, and gave me his number, the same one I'd known six years before. It never occurred to me that Earl still lived at 701 Robicheaux Street, Berwick, Louisiana—an address that would bring him great grief once the state and federal governments began totting up hurricane bills. For although he was a state charity case when the storm hit, all subsequent costs were managed as post-Katrina expenses, and only residents of New Orleans area zip codes qualified for continued coverage. After his treatment ended, it took several years and a good lawyer to release him from 1.3 million dollars of debt.

I called. He'd been alerted. "Hey," he said. "It's good to hear your voice." And then he commenced to tell how, after Katrina hit, he lay in Charity's ICU for four days, half-gone on morphine, taking forever to grasp the storm's power because it was "just one more hurricane" of the many he'd known. But after the lights failed for good and the food ran out, and addicts broke in through the flooded lower floors, and Earl's favorite nurse was found unconscious in a closet, having gobbled pills to kill the stress, he got it, and started lobbying for a way out. From what everyone had heard, Charity was the last hospital on the evacuation list. On day five, Earl, clad in a hospital gown and clutching his medical records in both hands, loped across Charity's roof to be whisked away by a navy Black Hawk. "When I looked down at New Orleans," he said, "all I saw was water."

. . .

In October, six weeks after I found Earl, I drove down from North Texas to visit him at Baton Rouge General. The nurse escorting me to his room happened to be Corey St. Pé, the son of Kerry St. Pé, executive director of the Barataria-Terrebonne National Estuary Program and a leading expert on water control and land loss in coastal Louisiana. If I hadn't known it before, I knew it now: south Louisiana is a small town.

Stopping just inside the door, I beheld my friend, swaddled in sheets like a small mummy, bald head poking out like a bulb. He raised himself slightly for a hug: his shoulders and back, through the sheets, were very warm; his cheek was cool and dry. He felt as light and portable as a doll.

Resuming our friendship was easy, even over the miles. On days when he was strong enough, we lingered on the phone, addressing favorite subjects: Cage, Takemitsu, and Messiaen; how to live as an artist in a consumer society; and memorable dishes like Chef John Folse's oyster-stuffed quail, savored at Bittersweet Plantation the year I visited Brownell Park for the travel story. Earl talked about the Atchafalaya constantly: the abundant native wildlife and plants, the depleted crawfish and cypress, government and industry roles in diminishing the rain forest. His home territory had always been a passion—now it was an obsession. As we continued talking, something in me sprang to life, a quickening of blood harking back perhaps, to Florida's Atlantic coast. Or was it just love of a single place, surfacing once more, as it did my last Wyoming winter? Or maybe, appreciation for a familiar environment conflated with appreciation of a friend. It didn't matter; it still doesn't. I wanted to respond, even if all I could do was bear witness.

* * *

When I first drove down to see Earl, I stayed with Dean and Natha an hour south of Baton Rouge in Bayou Sorrel. Their house was so firmly entrenched in the swamp even the chicken coop was built on stilts, and for good reason: it was about twenty feet from the thumb of a bayou, where alligators had been known to cruise. Inside the house, two caged parrots scolded furiously while the children's pet ferret darted among the furniture. I felt completely at home. Over wine and cheese Dean had brought from a trip back to Spain, we talked about the basin and its perilous state, Dean occasionally raising his voice like an evangelist. He and Natha took me on a swamp tour—the first of several, as it would turn out. I saw the beauty I remembered, as well as rusted, abandoned petroleum pumping stations and clear-cut cypress forests, naked but for their wretched stumps. "Maybe you could write about this," they said. I was already taking notes.

Still, there was the problem of where to start. What was the entry point? I needed an expert on the Atchafalaya—someone who knew it intimately and also had credence in the state's learned community. One afternoon a few weeks later, I happened to meet with a client in Houston, and after we finished up, I told her about my project and my search for an expert. She suggested I call her husband's cousin, Charles Chamberlain, historian for the Louisiana State Museum in New Orleans. I did. "That's easy," Charles said, when I posed my question. "You need to contact a guy named Earl Robicheaux."

· · ·

Earl's cancer required eight months of CHOP, a radical chemotherapy course combining three chemo drugs (cyclophosphamide, vincristine, and doxorubicin) and a steroid (prednisolone), in a cyclic regimen: one week on, three weeks off. He experienced the common side effects: a drop in blood counts, hair loss, and a sore mouth, plus night sweats, dizziness, and blackouts. He grew so fragile that in seven of eight breaks between treatments, he caught an infection, running dangerously high fevers that antibiotics can't always fix. During one zany phone conversation, I grew convinced he was hallucinating; Cage, Zappa, and Luc Ferrari were playing badminton with his brain cells. "Please, go to the hospital now, Earl," I said, but he refused the idea. It was already hard enough, he countered, getting friends and relatives to look in on Eula during his scheduled absences. "Do it anyway," I said. A few days later, he called from Baton Rouge. He'd finally begged a ride up to the hospital, where an orderly wheeled him into Emergency just in time. He had pneumonia, bad. If he'd waited another day, the doctors said, Earl might have died.

Earl underwent two surgeries, as well: one to remove the port in his head because the area was infected. (A port in his chest remained.) The other, toward the end of the regimen, involved an intestinal resectioning. The tumor there was gone, but the regimen had caused parts of his intestines to adhere to each other, blocking digestion.

For once in his life, Earl had stopped eating. "Definitely cause for alarm," he joked later.

Throughout this time, Earl continued as his mother's caregiver, relying on friends and family members to help out during his weeks in Baton Rouge General. I was never sure if Eula understood how ill her son was. A week after Earl had been diagnosed with pneumonia I called the house to see if he had come home. Eula said she didn't know when he'd return, but she'd heard he was "pretty bad."

In spring 2006, *Vanishing Wetlands* opened at the LSU Museum of Art in the Shaw Center for the Arts in Baton Rouge, and Earl attended in a wheelchair, "death warmed over," he said. Yet his CHOP regimen was almost done. In May, he checked into the Leonard J. Chabert Medical Center in Houma to begin eighteen months of "maintenance" chemo. His preliminary tests there revealed a new problem: brain lesions on both sides of his frontal lobe. He was told they were probably caused by the JC virus, common in the general population and sometimes linked to water quality. It springs to life when a person's immune system has been compromised. Now, Earl had an explanation for his occasional long-term memory loss, skewed sense of direction, and dizziness.

My friend chalked up his afflictions to bad luck, but I suspected more was at play, so during one visit to the Atchafalaya, I stopped by the New Iberia office of chemist, environmental activist, and MacArthur Fellow Wilma Subra, also a Berwick native. I asked if she thought Earl's conditions might be tied to pollution from the petroleum-related plants lining the Atchafalaya River and nearby bayous leading to the Gulf.

Subra cited Marine Shale and its oilfield waste incinerator in Amelia, a few miles from Berwick on Bayou Boeuf and a short walk from the old Thibodeaux property.

Set up in 1985 as a "recycling park," the facility became the largest hazardous waste incinerator in the world, its operators failing to control emissions and seemingly immune to compliance orders. Aggregate not incinerated was used as filler in community spaces like the Amelia Ball Park, Subra said. Many children and adults in Berwick and Morgan City got sick, some with cancer.

"Could Earl have been one of them?" I asked.

"We had an outbreak of neuroblastoma in the children," Subra replied, implying yes. "There was supposed to be one in the whole state, and we had eight. Most of them died."

Burkitt's is directly related to neuroblastoma. The treatment is the same.

Though a federal judge shut Marine Shale down in 1996, the waste continued to sit there, rotting.

"The waste is on the intercoastal," Subra said. "Every time there's a hurricane, some of it gets washed away. It's everywhere."

She guessed the waste could have caused Earl's brain lesions, too.

Between the Burkitt's and the brain lesions, Earl became eligible for disability payments, but since his lifetime earnings weren't high, neither were his monthly checks. Neither were Eula's Social Security benefits. The two lived frugally, grateful when a better-heeled relative dropped by to take them out to eat or proffer a holiday check. By the time the state granted them a home health assistant, Earl had gained back the weight he'd lost to cancer and a good deal more, because of inactivity and eating prepared foods. And he needed strong antidepressants to stay emotionally afloat, even though Zen, his soundscape work, and friends on the "outside" like Frédéric and John, kept him reasonably buoyant for a time. E-mail, the Internet, and an Amazon.com account also provided intellectual food and distraction. But years of isolation had taken a toll. His world was silting in.

.   .   .

In late May and early June 2006, I spent two weeks at Lake Fausse Point State Park thinking about water. How, when I was little, we drew it fresh and cool from the well at my grandfather McCutchan's Indiana farm, and slurped it from a tin dipper, drinking down the champagne of the earth. Or in my thirties, living one summer in my grandfather Bond's camp on Beech Hill Pond in Maine, bathing briskly each morning in the chilly, spring-fed lake, as he had, hollering with pleasure. Now, I was in my fifties, squatting on the bank of a Louisiana bayou from which I dared not drink, in which I dared not swim. I would not drink from the farm well, either—too many pesticides up there now. And the Beech Hill camp, erased from the ground by a relative and sold to a wealthy Bostonian, is home to daredevil motorboats, not the silent canoes my grandfather once made by hand.

One morning I reread Alan Watts's 1971 essay "The Watercourse Way," also a favorite of Earl's. It speaks of how wise it is to let a stream of water, or of life, go the way it is inclined to go. "The more I try to pin it down, the more it dissolves into streaming—into various kinds of pulsing and textures of tensing," Watts wrote.

> But this particular kind of tension against the stream is habitual, and the frustration which it engenders is chronic. If I believe that I would like to break a habit, that very wish is another form of tension, and this in turn is a form of the basic un-get-at-ability of It. We are all lunatics trying to stick pins into their own points, and it is thus that our frantic efforts to set the world to rights and to extend control over all happenings, inner and outer, are themselves the cause of most of our troubles. All force is tension against the stream.

One day I left the park and followed signs to a local pottery studio. I bought a hand-turned soup bowl, golden brown, flecked with brighter colors, and the right size for a hearty helping of gumbo. That night, I dreamed I was looking out over the Atchafalaya and saw honeyed lights, like puffs of goldenrod hovering over the land and waterscape, and I couldn't tell, exactly, what was beneath them, land or water. Then the golden puffs melted, and I saw men and women in saffron work clothing, tilling land, as in a Dutch painting, yet these weren't round Dutch figures but lean, tanned people, with hoes and rakes, working emerging soil, a land of low yellow grasses. I wrote in a notebook:

> It was clear that the land was theirs, and they knew how to perform wise stewardship. Though the grass was not green, there was a feeling of goodness. Perhaps the people were reviving the land, stimulating it with their rakes and hoes, singing to it. The only dots of color besides gold: a bit of blue or green from a shirt collar, a neckerchief. Like the bowl I found yesterday. Exactly like that bowl.

CHAPTER 10

State
of the Basin

One week in June, two years later, I
left the same cabin at Lake Fausse
Point and drove around the basin
searching for unsentimental por-
trayals of the swamps. I needed to do it,
I thought, or risk any credibility as an
objective observer. I needed to remove
my gold-colored glasses.

My first stop was the Butte La Rose
home of Jim Delahoussaye, who I found
relaxing in his wide-windowed living
room, facing a thriving garden with
noisy, occupied birdhouses and a view
of the water. Jim, who had already

shared with me knowledge about the "old days" with the Myette Point community, and his family's deep French and Acadian roots around St. Martinville, poured me a cool glass of tea at his kitchen table and offered to reflect on the basin. When I asked him about its special character, he sat up straight and delivered a brisk assessment of what was, and is.

"There *was* an essence to the basin," he said. "And it was composed of what it was then. It was the water, it was the open river, the bayous, the fish, the birds, all of that. But it isn't the same anymore, and you can't re-create it. That's why I say I have so little patience for people who want to preserve the basin. That's fine—that's well and good. But take it as it is. Don't require it to be what it used to be.

"All of those old things we talk about—the trees, the open water, the flow—all of that—it's like remembering a person who's grown old. It's still that same person, but it's not the same as it was when it was young, you know?

"There are people who are very famous, well-known photographers in the basin, whom I won't name. And I'm probably the only person who's ever told those people, face-to-face, that I didn't like their photographs. Because they just show something pretty. But that isn't all it was. It was dangerous. It smelled bad. You could die out there. It wasn't *hard* to die out there. There was death after death after death that had to do with the character of the environment. And it wasn't just the natural environment—it was the people, too. If you did the wrong thing, you could get shot—and people did get shot!"

I agreed with Jim: you can't go back to what was. And no one, not even the most entrenched sentimentalist, honestly believes it's possible, or even desirable at this point, to restore the Atchafalaya Basin to what it used to be. The best anyone can do is support stewardship for what exists now. That's a tall order, though, because the basin will ultimately fill with sediment, although Jim pointed out that for a while, the gradual filling of lakes and even levee building created excellent shallow-water habitats for hunting and fishing. Sometimes transitions yield unexpected riches.

"There's a train that we all get on when we're born," Jim said. "And we sit in our boxcar as the train moves on, and when we die, we step off the train. But when we step off the train, it's not the same train as it was when we stepped on."

Then why, I asked, would you want to devote your retirement to writing a book about the way things aren't? Jim's face softened, and his voice lowered. Because, he replied, the children and grandchildren of the basin people have no idea what their elders were like, and "I want them to understand who they were.

"When the people of Myette Point were teaching me what they did so well, there was no way I could pay them back for their patience. But I could write. This is a way of paying them back, for what they did for me, forty years ago."

Paying back, paying forward, leaving a legacy. Noble impulses born of intimacy with someone or something. I wondered, as I took leave of Jim, if such callings will die out with the generations behind us, and the specificities of our lives will go unrecorded. But doesn't every generation fear its story will sink to the bottom forever?

* * *

Ruminating thus, I drove east on I-10 to Baton Rouge, to speak to biologist and hydrologist Charlie Demas, director of the USGS Louisiana Water Science Center. The U.S. Geological Survey is one of three major federal players in the Atchafalaya region (the other two being the Army Corps and the U.S. Fish and Wildlife Service) and is a nonregulatory agency, providing scientific data and studies to other federal, state, and local agencies. Here, I thought, I'd drown dreams of family fishing communities and home-grown food with a stiff drink of science.

It was easy to locate the USGS office in a tan, open-air complex behind the Capital City Grill on the north side of Baton Rouge. Though the doors facing the parking lot bore little identification, I guessed correctly that the SUV with the canoe on top pointed to USGS, and, it turned out, the car and canoe were Demas's. In a generous conference room, on two wide tables, Demas spread several maps and books for me to peruse. When I asked him to describe the basin's condition now, he expanded, in more technical terms, on Jim Delahoussaye's sentiments.

"It's an impaired ecosystem, but it's a functioning ecosystem, and it's also an ecosystem that includes the human component," he said. "It is very much utilized by Louisiana. It's a very important resource both from an ecological standpoint and through a cultural and economic standpoint. And I think that is something that the rest of the country has to understand.

"Ultimately, if man weren't around, and the Mississippi River had changed its course and gone down the Atchafalaya, the swamp would be bottomland hardwood. The new swamp would be forming further south in a new delta that would be created. That being said, the impact of humans on the basin has been to accelerate that ecological succession.

"The basin is filling in because of our hydrologic modifications," Demas stated. "We need energy to transport sediment, and if you stop that energy, either by blocking a natural channel or by routing it into open water, you're reducing the available energy, which means the sediment is going to drop out. Now, we've got all that oil and gas exploration, all the timber cutting, even the local or commercial fisherman who says, Hey, I want a better channel into my honey hole. He cuts it. *Damn, it's filling in faster and I can't figure out why.* Well, you've got sediment-laden water flowing into zero-velocity water. What happens? It drops out, folks."

I examined the historical maps Demas gestured toward, noting how the lakes and rivers had gradually shriveled over time: healthy, pumping hearts and arteries gone to spider veins. Although he didn't name them, I gathered government-sponsored modifications like levees, channel dredging, and Old River Control were greatly responsible for, as Earl has described it, "performing too many surgeries on the patient."

I asked for more details, and Demas continued. "It used to be that when water went overbank [as in a flood], you had a natural levee and the water flowed through the trees. Most of the deposition was through the trees. Not anymore. With the spoil banks, channel training work, and the head cutting in the bed (the main channel is getting deeper), we need a higher stage to get it overbanked than we used to. Therefore, the water doesn't return as efficiently as before, which means more of the sediment drops out.

"I can take you places where water will flow east, west, north, and south depending on what the stage is. In part that's due to the deferential deposition that's been created by, let's say, the oil and gas canal that cuts off a bayou. Or a logging trail. It's not just the oil and gas guys that did this. Everybody who's used the basin has had an impact on it. You know that *Pogo* statement: we have met the enemy, and he is us.

"What we're trying to do now is slow the process down to the pace that should have been," Demas said. "The major management philosophy is to get as much fresh water as possible in the back swamp areas with an appropriate amount of sediment."

Charlie Demas came to Baton Rouge from northern California after the 1973 flood—the one that washed the last basin dwellers over the levees and proved Old River Control insufficient, when a sixty-seven-foot-high concrete guide wing at the Low Sill Structure was destroyed. (Emergency repairs held it all together; by 1979 an auxiliary structure was authorized, and in 1986, completed.) Demas has monitored water quality and sediment in the basin primarily south of I-10. He's observed, for instance, an accretion problem. As more silt settled in the basin, the ground elevation rose, creating a need for higher levees. Higher ground elevation also weakened the Atchafalaya's capacity to handle a catastrophic flood. In *Designing the Bayous,* his thorough, invaluable history of water control in the Atchafalaya Basin, Martin Reuss described the Corps of Engineers' proposed remedy to continue deepening the Atchafalaya River's main channel to increase flow capacity and take on more sediment. At the same time, they would close more distribution channels and extend the East Protection Levee downstream. By shrinking the system, the Corps thought, the natural riverbanks would build up and the levees wouldn't have to be heaped so high.

While this plan promised more efficient flood control, it exacerbated another problem. High spoil banks—already piling up from the Corps' canal dredging projects, were preventing the annual high water from replenishing the swampland and threatening water quality and vegetation, fish, and wildlife downstream. For example, class 1 cypress, the most durable and desirable species, requiring dry conditions for germination, had already thinned out from an increase in standing water caused by spoil banks. Commercially important fish and shrimp species were suffering. Demas noted that the mussel population has receded dramatically in some areas since he moved to the area.

In addition, invasive plants were clogging the swamp, and the problem continues.

"To me, all the work we're doing out there will be for naught if we don't get a handle on the invasive plant species," Demas told me. "There are areas where the salvinia mat is so thick, bank to bank, grass is growing on it. Well, it doesn't matter how much you restore the hydrology—if we can't control those plant species, there still won't be any oxygen under the water. Then we have the invasive fish species. You know we've got bigheaded carp, grass carp, silver carp, and others. If people would eat more silver carp and some of the other invasive fish, we'd be better off. A lot of invasive species in this system come from upriver—thanks to those nice folks in Arkansas or to the navigation industry via the Great Lakes."

I understood that together, siltation, blocked natural distributaries, invasive plant species, and waste-producing shortcuts have given the Atchafalaya Basin an acute case of constipation. Even the new delta in Atchafalaya Bay bears an unusual profile. Though natural in shape, it did not emerge via normal sheet flooding but as, essentially, a sediment trap.

•   •   •

Prompted by legislation like the Water Quality Act of 1965 and the public's increasing fears for the basin's legendary fishing and hunting grounds, the Army Corps produced several environmental impact statements, including a feasibility study in 1982, which Demas described as a master plan for the basin. The U.S. Fish and Wildlife Service was busy, too. In 1978, it proposed to establish a fish, wildlife, and multiuse area in the basin. But obstacles lay everywhere, and still do. Private landowners, who own more than half the floodway, and petroleum companies, who would preserve their water routes to the sea (and their contracts with the Army Corps), work hard to protect their interests.

In response to what was, at the very least, a public relations crisis, the Greater Atchafalaya Basin Council formed in the early 1960s to provide a platform for public discussion and serve as an official body to work with government agencies (all told, the Army Corps of Engineers, U.S. Fish and Wildlife, the U.S. Geological Survey, the Louisiana Department of Natural Resources, the Louisiana State Department of Fish and Wildlife, and Louisiana State University) toward policies and solutions amenable to all. Since then, interests and responsibilities have danced within various other planning and advisory bodies. The fine details, jingling with acronyms, have been well documented by Martin Reuss.

By 1985, the Corps had been authorized $250 million to preserve and restore the basin ecosystem—not enough for a transformation, but useful. For a while the Corps' work was hampered by the state's slow response. But in 1999, Louisiana adopted a fifteen-year master plan drawn up by a seventy-five-member committee representing all interest groups in the basin, including the Corps; its implementation would be overseen by the Louisiana Department of Natural Resources. Today, LDNR works with annual plans for specific projects in the basin.

Lately the Army Corps has been designing freshwater diversion structures, including sediment traps, to help refresh the swamps. Buffalo Cove, Demas said, contains several of these projects. At one time, two channels ran through the lake, serving as drains and providing water to the interior swamp. But by 1995, Buffalo Cove had almost filled in. The older channel is completely filled, leaving a single channel that is mostly filled during low flow. At low stage, no water flows in or out of the swamp.

"Therefore, the swamp doesn't drain very well," Demas said. "Because of constant inundation the trees are always stressed, with little regeneration of cypress and other trees in the (semipermanently) flooded areas of the swamp." Today, young willows stand along the old channel, indicating recent disturbance or sedimentation. Behind them, the canopy rises taller and taller. The trees' ages indicate when the disturbance first occurred.

"If it's a mature willow, it's probably been there forty to sixty years—the life expectancy of a willow," Demas said. "Willow would also show up on the spoil banks when you build a pipeline canal. That's not necessarily a sediment disturbance. It's a disturbance to the hydrology. But in either case, you've opened up the canopy. So who's going to come in first?"

I'd seen such disturbances on outings with Dean Wilson, who is probably the most outspoken environmentalist in the basin. Whether the guests on his swamp trips are regular tourists or snoops like me, he makes sure to point out—in addition to the wedge-tailed cormorants and loopy, roseate spoonbills—the willows, the spoil banks, and the defunct oil and gas pipes still striking unnatural poses in the arrow-straight canals dug to accommodate them. Dean is not a lone wolf though, as some would paint him, but a team player. For example, in 2009, he, along with the Louisiana Crawfish Producers Association, sued a private landowner who had installed a dam and pumping station for a hunting club at Lost Lake. The structure blocked public access and violated federal environmental laws, altering the lake's natural flow and interfering with fish migration. Crawfishermen had noticed the dam in 2006, and the Army Corps addressed the case a year later, issuing a cease-and-desist order against the landowner. Dean and the CPA provided the final push required to get the dam and pumping station removed.

Dean has questioned the sediment accumulating in the Corps' sediment traps. Where will *that* go? Charlie Demas admits it has to be dumped somewhere, but on land that's going to turn terrestrial anyway. The sediment might be put back into the river for coastal land building or, if that isn't feasible, in areas that are already high, as higher ground provides refuge for animals during floods. Despite the running questions, Dean Wilson and Charlie Demas agree quite often. And both are looking just as closely at what's gone right as at what's gone wrong. Both mentioned to me the regeneration on the northeast arm of Murphy Lake, south of Baton Rouge.

"There's a trail cut through the cypress by commercial fishermen," Demas said. "It's only as wide as a crawfish boat. It looks like you're going through a cathedral—it's really beautiful. We're intrigued with it because it has such great regeneration." When I asked why the trail fared so well, Demas answered, "No one seems to know."

●   ●   ●

As for water quality, Demas said the basin has not been EPA compliant, "because during the summer, it naturally goes to zero dissolved oxygen in those backwater areas." In addition, Henderson Swamp, which the I-10 elevated highway cuts across, is under a mercury advisory. But the rest of the basin isn't, and Demas thinks it's partly because of the swamps' river connection. "We see low mercury values in the Mississippi and Atchafalaya river main channels. Basically, I think the connection to the Atchafalaya decreases the period during which the water conditions in the basin are favorable for the methylation of mercury" (methyl mercury being the form of mercury that accumulates in the environment).

Although the Department of Environmental Quality has been working to meet federal standards here, it has proposed to modify those standards to fit "the reality" of the basin's condition, meaning the reality of its users and Mother Nature. "The dissolved-oxygen standards are violated in the isolated areas of the swamp on a regular basis," Demas said. "However, these low DO values are a result of natural processes that occur in any swamp during low-water periods. Hence the call to modify the criteria."

And so goes the dance, set to music that changes every few beats, because, it appears, many people operate the CD player, and the damaged disc is likely to skip anyway. Still, Charlie Demas thinks the nongovernmental organizations, state and federal agencies work fairly well together on management and scientific issues.

"But we don't feel we're moving fast enough, and I think everybody has that frustration. We don't assign fault—who knows whose fault it is? We have a technical advisory group that DNR formed, and there's the technical group that works with the Army Corps—and we're all the same players. Some of us have cycled through several groups at both the Corps and the state."

It seemed clear, from my conversations with Demas and other state and federal managers that they've all been trying valiantly, for years, to push a boulder up a mountain. Yet in conversations with basin area residents, I found it nearly impossible to find a private citizen who did not refer to the Army Corps in less than a derisive tone. The truth is, local interests for fish, wildlife, and environmental conservation are very often incompatible with flood control and broader commercial interests, which the Corps, for all recent claims to ecological fidelity, represents to many people. And even among commercial interests, there are conflicts, like the case at Lost Lake. Charlie Demas offered another, theoretical example: while increased flooding in an area could increase a fisherman's seasonal catch, it could restrict a timber company's access to trees. Just as the basin is cross-hatched with waterways, so is it cross-hatched with interests.

And so our meeting ended. It was late afternoon, and Demas would soon be out the door, perhaps to launch his canoe in the basin and throw out a line, just to relax. If there is one thing the basin's managers have in common, it's a personal attachment to the environment. They're either born here and stay, or come from the outside and don't want to leave. Their boots are muddy, seven days a week.

· · ·

As I left Baton Rouge, I felt the intermittent breeze of decline playing at my ears. "Here is Jim Delahoussaye writing about a dying culture," I said to my windshield, "and Charlie Demas and his colleagues delaying, less efficiently than they'd like, the death of the natural system that gave birth to that culture." I wondered how anyone could summon the optimism required for a Save the Basin campaign. My honeyed glasses were dissolving, as if they'd soaked in Henderson Swamp for a year.

I nearly canceled my last visit, with Lamar Hale, Atchafalaya Basin project manager for the U.S. Army Corps of Engineers. I'd be better off, I thought, sneaking back to Lake Fausse Point and communing with the gator who surfaced beneath my cabin deck each evening. I'd even have time for a short hike. I could watch the wild rabbits feeding in the little green meadow by the water and salute the barred owls whose eyes seemed to brush my neck every time I traipsed around their bend in the path.

But I resisted the urge and went on to New Orleans.

The next morning I presented myself at the Corps' New Orleans District headquarters, a white, corporate-style complex along the Mississippi, and, coincidentally, three blocks from the double-shotgun house where Earl lived in his early thirties. On the central building's first floor, where I presented my visitor's badge, I noticed hand-sanitizer dispensers stationed prominently in corners where once, freestanding, sand-filled canister ashtrays might have stood. I trailed the dispensers to the third floor and Hale's cubicle, which was fit to burst with maps, papers, and books. On a shelf over his computer, he had pressed a yellow sticky note bearing the Hindu spiritual greeting: *Namaste*.

. . .

Hale, a genial, soft-spoken man, invited me to lunch in the Corps cafeteria, where other employees were watching a live broadcast of President Obama, in town that day to visit the Katrina-whipped Lower Ninth Ward and conduct a town hall at the University of New Orleans. As we settled in with our sandwiches, Hale, no doubt used to being a spokesman, volunteered his mission: "My motivation is a love for the Atchafalaya Basin and to try to do good things with taxpayer dollars—the most and best I can with what Congress gives me."

I knew he really meant it. As he told his story, his affection for the Atchafalaya Basin became clear.

A Texan by birth, Hale began working in the basin in 1973, managing survey projects for companies that did contract work for the Army Corps. For more than ten years, he moved around—to Denver, Austin (his hometown), and Richmond—according to the company he was based with, but he was often assigned to work in the basin. When the economy tanked in the mid-1980s, he returned to LSU, where he'd earned his master's degree, and began work toward a Ph.D. in civil engineering. For his dissertation project, he proposed mapping the entire basin, using the new Geographical Information System (GIS) software, some of it developed by the Army Corps for military purposes. "I thought, if I'm going to start over, I'm going to retrain myself," Hale told me.

Hale knew the Army Corps retained a stash of reports and surveys of the basin—he'd been involved with some of them. Their accuracy depended on surveyors who periodically walked (or paddled) lines from one side to the other, up and down the basin, measuring the elevation of land and depth of water. All told, there were about thirty-five separate surveys, some covering the entire basin, others particular ranges. (The last cross-basin surveys, Hale said, were conducted near Morgan City in the early 1990s. To save money, the Corps switched to aerial surveys.) But no one had analyzed the information comprehensively, and Hale saw a chance to incorporate it in a study that showed changes in the basin over time. He also developed three-dimensional GIS programs that gave the measurements more impact. Not surprisingly, his study showed both land accretion and bank erosion. The basin was changing rapidly.

Hale finished his work in the mid-1980s, around the time the Corps received the $250 million restoration purse for land purchase, flood-control projects, water management, and other initiatives. It desperately needed someone around like Hale, who knew the basin very, very well.

"One thing led to another, and when I got out of school, the Corps said, well, why don't you come down here and work out of our offices?" Though still technically employed as a research engineer by LSU, Hale pitched his tent in New Orleans. (It wasn't until after Hurricane Katrina that he was officially hired by the Corps.)

One of the Corps' new mandates was to restore the basin's historical flow, and in 1996, when Governor Mike Foster named the Department of Natural Resources as lead state agency on the project, work began. One pilot project connected with restored flow is the Buffalo Cove site Charlie Demas looks after. But, I gathered from Hale's comments, restoration efforts have amounted to too little, too late.

"Today, all we have are the remnants of lakes and some back areas," Hale said. "And we still have had to dredge the main channel of the Atchafalaya in the Morgan City area a lot, year-round, because of the accumulated sediment." Even the commercial road to the sea is endangered.

Hale cited another tricky issue: the question of authority over Atchafalaya land. Generations ago, when the U.S. government decided the river would be handmaiden to the Mississippi, it sold off swamplands to finance levee construction. Investors included timber companies that clear-cut the forests. But there were smaller players, too: farmers who bought modest tracts on higher ground—forty, eighty, one hundred acres—and much of that land remains in the families today, with dozens of heirs, each owning a little piece. If the government wishes to buy land for conservation, it faces lengthy negotiations, assuming all family members are speaking to one another. Hale says a recent program to buy seventy thousand acres worked out well, partly because the land they sought meant little to the owners.

"All the old timber's gone, and the good timber lands stay flooded with bad water most of the time so the timber doesn't grow real fast," he said. "With this program, the landowners got to maintain their mineral rights, so it was a win-win."

Seventy thousand acres is just a sliver of the basin, though. And commercial interests aren't going to devote their property to conservation anytime soon.

Lamar Hale reminded me that, as the basin fills, the Atchafalaya is extending itself, moving out into the Gulf, creating new land. The new Atchafalaya Delta is one of only two places along Louisiana's delicate coastline where land is building, not disappearing, and it wouldn't be happening if the Army Corps hadn't previously manicured the river's main channel. The second land-building scene is the previously mentioned Wax Lake Delta, formed after a relief canal was dredged off the Atchafalaya to keep Morgan City from flooding. Receiving about one-third the Atchafalaya's flow at the Wax Lake Outlet Control Structure, Wax Lake began, predictably, to fill with sediment, and the new delta surfaced after the 1973 flood. By 2005, you could walk across what used to be Wax Lake and with good binoculars, glimpse the new delta, stretching five miles out into the Gulf. Because it has remained untouched since the 1941 dredging, it stands as a model for land growth in the region. Some experts propose creating another Atchafalaya delta, diverted east toward the ailing Barataria and Terrebonne basins, where Louisiana's coastal land loss is the worst. Others recommend releasing water from the Mississippi itself to carry sediment, via spriglike deltas, closer to New Orleans.

Hale questions these ideas. "It comes back to the availability of the sediment and how much water the river can provide to move it. We have to find a way to preserve the existing wetlands, too, of replenishing and nurturing them. I don't want to sound like doom and gloom, but I think it's just a losing battle."

I looked around the Corps cafeteria and counted about a dozen employees lingering over dessert—just a few of the hundreds working in this single facility, from the cafeteria cook, a dreadlocked man with a hairnet who joshed with every customer and built sandwiches rivaling Central Grocery's muffalettas, to scientists and managers like Hale, who oversee employees in and out of the field, report to and confer with higher-ups, and serve on advisory committees for several other agencies. When Hale and I returned to his cubicle, he handed me several maps and plans, including proposals I knew were years in the making and more years in passing and implementing. Suddenly I grasped the immense

contraption that is the Army Corps' system, its burdensome responsibility, and its power. It's likely, I decided, that the Corps, together with
the other interests and agencies in the Atchafalaya, is as clogged as the
basin, Louisiana's ailing patient—now, it would seem, on life support.

"We have met the enemy, and he is us," quoth Charlie Demas.

"It's not the same train as it was when we stepped on," said Jim
Delahoussaye.

"*Namaste*," Lamar Hale wrote on a sticky note, eye level over his
desk.

CHAPTER 11

Turning Tides

In February 2007, *Voices of the Atch-afalaya*, the exhibit containing John Amrhein's fifty-nine black-and-white photographs and Earl's sixty-minute soundscape, opened in the Patterson museum. Friends, relatives, and St. Mary Parish residents thronged the exhibit hall, sipping wine and Coke from plastic cups, lingering longer before each photograph than city gallery hoppers are wont to do. Dean Wilson and Natha Booth manned an information table, passing out literature for Basinkeepers. Eula attended, escorted by a nephew, and watched the proceedings from a chair off to one side. "A lot of people came," she said to me, nodding.

But stealing the show were the subjects, attired for the evening in crisp dresses or shirts and jackets, listening to their own voices resound through the space, staring with pride and wonder at John's haunting images of themselves landing fish, peeling shrimp, gigging frogs, and even, in the case of boat pilot Shine Beadle, showing off his violin, whose wobbly sound haunts Earl's soundscape like an old 78-rpm record. Adam Morales, a veteran fisherman and as yet unrecognized driftwood sculpture artist, wandered the hall, appraising its arrangement, not knowing that in two years, the American Visionary Art Museum in Baltimore would select his *Statue of Liberty* as the icon for a year-long international exhibition titled "Life, Liberty, and the Pursuit of Happiness." Across the room from Morales, the elderly shrimper Marvin Hardee posed for snapshots before his own picture, his mouth twisted upward into a little smile when viewers did a double-take passing by. In one evening, he had turned into a living legend.

Earl's notes for the show read, in part:

> Photographs capture history and tell stories—they are vehicles by which we know ourselves. The sounds recorded for the accompanying "soundscape" are derived directly from the river as source material—ferry engines, bells, fog horns, whistles, seagulls, bridge sounds, tug boats and trains provide an ambient soundfield for the emergence of voices of our elder residents. The voices tell stories based on memory and, in so doing, create impressions or feelings. The idea the composer would like to convey is "the river as keeper of dreams." The impermanence of the river, constant—yet flowing, is much like our subconscious itself.

In three years' time, five of the twelve men and women featured in the show would be gone, entombed in nearby cemeteries. In October 2009 both John and I happened to be in town shortly after Shine Beadle's death, and with Earl, attended his Masonic funeral service at a Morgan City funeral home. The sanctuary was packed with at least four generations, the elderly parked closest to the coffin in wheelchairs, the most restless children sent to the lobby to play. The Masonic service begins with a solemn procession of the brotherhood, wearing over their suits the traditional white apron, symbolizing the Freemason's trade and innocence. On their lapels, the men wear evergreen sprigs, for faith in the soul's immortality. Shine Beadle's rites were based in Christian practice, according to the tradition of his lodge. Toward the end, everyone present joined in the Lord's Prayer, and the fisherman was committed to the Celestial Lodge above.

* * *

Also in 2007, Earl received a commission from Dolores Henderson, beloved Morgan City educator of at-risk children and a well-known storyteller; some of her tales have been documented by folklore scholars. Titled *Miss Toots,* Earl's CD, composed of six autobiographical narratives, blends Henderson's smooth, lyrical voice with nature utterances, piano/bass jazz, and improvised percussive effects with found sounds like a player piano, a washing machine, and a spinning bicycle wheel. Together, they yield an organic whole—a kind of sound poem. Henderson's opening narrative is based on Louisiana childhood memories, but the best sections may be her long remembrances of David Butler and Royal Robertson, the outsider artists Frédéric Allamel introduced to Earl. Henderson, like Butler and Robertson, is African American and had known both artists personally, even commissioning them. "They're special people with a spiritual connection to their maker, and a love of their fellow man—but wanting as much privacy as possible," she says on the CD.

Henderson had gotten to know David Butler through his niece, who worked in the cafeteria of the school where Henderson taught. She photographed him with his work and created a scrapbook to take to classes, "so children would know there was somebody in Louisiana who became famous because he made art from nothing—a black man who made art from nothing, and has pieces in the Smithsonian." Of Royal Robertson, Henderson said, "He had his own little connection to the universe. He used to say he dreamed a lot of the things he painted—or got messages from the Bible."

According to Henderson, Butler and Robertson's lives changed when art collectors discovered them and talked them into selling their work. Butler grew sad, and his bright palette darkened. Robertson, who was delusional and given to ranting, was sure the men buying his galactic paintings were using them on TV science fiction programs and getting rich. "It had to be a busy head, with all the thoughts that came from him," Henderson said. "If people really knew him, they wouldn't say what they do about the man."

On the track devoted to Robertson, Henderson's voice is backed with up-tempo piano/bass jazz by Earl and Bill Hunszinger and interrupted sporadically by "Lumpy" Wayne Barrow, Brownell Park's former landscaper, hollering, imitating Robertson:

Who is that?
Ain't nobody home!
I think they're scared!
They're scared of me—
they think something might happen!
They got to put their mind on something.
They got to put their mind in the wind!
I'll put their mind in the wind!

Though locals say Barrow sounds exactly like the artist, Earl pointed out that "Put your mind in the wind" is a Wayne Barrow original. "He said that to me at the park, all the time."

*   *   *

In 2008, Earl's interests began to migrate from the basin to Louisiana's melting coastline. Since *Voix des Marecages* and the *Marsh Mission* project, he had several times revisited Isle de Jean Charles and Point Aux Chenes to check on the deteriorating conditions there. One day, we took his truck down each of the five roads that finger out from the city of Houma to Bayous du Large, Grand Caillou, Petit Caillou, Terrebonne, and Point Aux Chenes, toward Caillou and Terrebonne Bays, east of the Atchafalaya. Each road ends at, or vanishes into, marsh or water. At Point Aux Chenes, I was prepared to see the lush oaks Mike Tidwell described in his 2003 book *Bayou Farewell,* but all I saw was a wasteland of water, marsh, and dead or dying trees. "I mean, there are NO good oaks here," I wrote in my notebook. The road descended into the water, like a boat launch. All we saw were rock piles, rundown fishing boats, and a couple of pickup trucks, their occupants—several men and a woman—standing by their cabs, drinking beer. Overlooking the scene was a tilted statue of Christ, its white robe flaking off in the wind.

From there we drove to the Isle de Jean Charles Marina to grab a cold drink and say hello to Earl's friend Theo Chaisson, the owner and proprietor. Theo's marina, perched high over a bayou, looked new and smelled of fresh-sawn timber, as the deck, roof, and some walls, smashed by Hurricane Rita, had recently been replaced. Earl was uncomfortable going in at first, remembering that the last time he stopped by, he didn't have money to pay for his Coke and Theo had given it to him anyway.

A blue-eyed, olive-skinned man with curly black hair springing from a dredging company gimme cap, Theo was glad to see Earl and happy to meet me, since Earl introduced me as a Louisiana fan ("She's from Texas," he added, a little apologetically). But I perceived then, as I have on other occasions in the "Sportsman's Paradise," that I might not take part in their conversation, only stand by politely and listen. Earl told me that once, a woman curator at a state museum questioned his paucity of female oral-history sources, and he replied, "That's because the men do all the talking in this culture; the women either don't or won't talk. They defer to their husbands." While I hadn't found that to be true, I understood Earl's focus on documenting traditionally male pursuits, like hunting and fishing, and my position as an outsider to that world.

Out on the deck, Earl, Theo, and two men, a tall one in Dickies overalls and a short one in a FedEx driver's shirt, drank Dr. Pepper and talked about land loss. The tall man in Dickies dominated, complaining about the uneven post-Rita resources given to the communities along the five roads coming down from Houma. The others agreed, speculating on what might have happened with the funding. Finally, the man in Dickies drew up to full height and cleared his throat. "Look," he said, "if you have five children, and a pot of white beans, you don't give some to some children and none to the others!" The hand holding his Dr. Pepper can ladled beans into the free palm. Everyone nodded. There was nothing more to say.

Looking out past the deck, I noted the storm-ravaged houses and camps: the worst I'd seen in the area, and uninhabitable, by most standards. Yet as Earl and I left the marina and crept along the road, we watched people enter and exit these battered shacks and trailers in normal fashion, as if their homes didn't list on stilts, their unscreened windows weren't open to dirt and mosquitoes on a hot day. I gasped at one utterly wrecked dwelling bearing a new house number, though I'd seen houses like this when I toured St. Bernard Parish, post-Katrina. Isle de Jean Charles is one of several communities vulnerable to any storm shearing the coast, and though it may lie on what feels like the last stop before the end of the world, the majority of the seventy-eight families remaining there in 2009 still thought of it as a fine place to build, and rebuild. No one could miss the residents' will to permanency here.

* * *

Not long after that outing, Earl received support from the Louisiana Sea Grant College Program and the Louisiana State Museum to create a CD documenting Grand Isle, Louisiana's only inhabited barrier island. Lying directly south of New Orleans on the southern tip of Louisiana 1, the 6.1-square-mile wand of land juts northeast into Barataria Bay and receives a direct hit from a hurricane about once every seven years, with countless indirect hits between. Combined with slow-onset land loss from erosion and subsidence, severe storms have steadily eaten away at Grand Isle. When in 2003 the USGS reported that Louisiana had lost approximately nineteen hundred square miles of coastal land in the twentieth century, and would lose another seven hundred over the next fifty years if new restoration was not accomplished quickly, Grand Isle residents began to believe their grandchildren would never set foot there, because Grand Isle would lie underwater.

Grand Isle's disappearance would also mean losing a place laden with storied history, beginning with the Chitimacha and subsequent European settlement. In the early 1800s, it was a home to the pirate Jean Lafitte, and by midcentury, large plantations sprawled all over it. After the Civil War, it became a popular summer watering hole for wealthy families, who stayed in cottages (some of them renovated slave cabins) and new hotels.

Grand Isle is also the primary setting for Kate Chopin's 1899 novel *The Awakening*. In this once-controversial work, the protagonist, Edna Pontellier, struggles against constraining societal roles to discover her intense sexual drive and her need to live a more unconventional life separate from her husband and children. Part of her awakening involves embracing self-expression through art and acknowledging the solitude an artistic calling requires.

In the book's final scene, on the beach at Grand Isle, Edna decides to abandon the barriers to her authenticity:

> The water of the Gulf stretched out before her, gleaming with the million lights of the sun. The voice of the sea is seductive, never ceasing, whispering, clamoring, murmuring, inviting the soul to wander in abysses of solitude. All along the white beach, up and down, there was no living thing in sight. A bird with a broken wing was beating the air above, reeling, fluttering, circling disabled down, down to the water.

Edna removes her clothes ("How strange and awful it seemed to stand naked under the sky! How delicious!") and walks into the sea. She begins to swim, not looking back. She swims and swims, heading toward the distance. Now she hears the voice of her confidante, Madame Reisz, the unmarried pianist who marked the resolve necessary to go her own way ("And you call yourself an artist! What pretensions, Madame! The artist must possess the courageous soul that dares and defies!"). She swims farther and farther, exhausting herself. The last sounds Edna hears are voices from earlier days: her father and sister, the barking of an old dog chained to a tree, the clanging spurs of a cavalry officer, the purr of bees. Whether Edna's suicide is read as victory or defeat, it is accompanied by aural memories representing past and present.

In composing *Grand Isle Diaries* (subtitled *Vanishing Coast, Vanishing Culture: An Environmental Oral History-Soundscape of Grand Isle and Cheniere Caminada, Louisiana*) Earl took a similar approach to sound, opening with a twenty-first-century hurricane rescue helicopter beating its way over the island, followed by the (now-deceased) marsh buggy driver and alligator hunter Dovie Naquin from Point Aux Chenes, singing in shaky, but insistent tones, a harmonically and rhythmically wayward song Earl thinks "Mr. Dovie" might have made up.

> *If you really want a Loosiana Cajun man*
> *You gotta know how to handle that man*
> *If you don't know how to handle that man*
> *You better go and run just as fast as you can*
> *He's a good old workin' man*
> *He can make his living on the sea*
> *Or he can make his living on the land*
> *But you can't hold his hand all the time*
> *You got to let him go*
> *He gonna make one or two runs in town*
> *He gonna come back to you just as fast as he can*
> *That's a Loosiana Cajun man*

When the song is complete, it loops back, but softly, like a dancing ghost, accompanying residents' stories about ancestors who farmed and fished the island. About midway through the track, an accordion begins pumping in the background, out of sync with the singer, adding to the disjointed, dreamlike atmosphere.

In his liner notes, Earl named artist Joseph Cornell his inspiration. "His boxed constructions appear to me as diaries—a remembrance, a keeper of dreams, and as such, a barometer of change." And indeed, in the tracks that follow, Earl's oral diarists remember a lot: menacing mosquito swarms, feisty tales of Jean Lafitte, the wonders of island birding, and more. In one eerie segment, Earl layers frightening hurricane stories over the ominous tolling of a church bell and a TV broadcast of the pope celebrating Mass. The bell is a local treasure: it hangs in Our Lady of the Isle, Grand Isle's Catholic church, and originally hung in adjacent Cheniere Caminida's church until the great October storm of 1893 wiped out that community. Earl says pirates brought the bell to Westwego, on the Mississippi's west bank across from New Orleans, where it was buried in a cemetery. Eventually it was discovered and brought to Grand Isle, and a tower was built for it in 1961. Earl admits there are other versions of that story, too.

Perhaps the most moving piece on the CD is a seventeen-minute meditation on coastal land loss, in which Earl layered citizens' reflections over rolling surf and wailing gulls. Nearly everyone believes Grand Isle will be submerged one day, perhaps as soon as a generation or two from now. The final speaker, Frédéric Allamel, reads Earl's poem "Clouds of Time" in French. The last six lines express a disappearing community's grief:

> *Our souls thirst for liberation*
> *with death upon us we will be*
> *set free, one by one, yet together*
> *our souls will rise once again*
>
> *And we will again be set adrift*
> *Passing, like clouds of time.*

In Frédéric's dolorous French intonation, the poem's meaning is clear and powerful. At its completion, a soprano singing Puccini's lush, melancholy aria "O mio babbino caro" (Oh My Dear Papa) floats in over the water, and when the final lines ("Babbo, pieta, pieta" [Oh God, I would want to die!]) fade, the ocean continues alone.

Grand Isle Diaries will be part of a traveling exhibit mounted by the Louisiana State Museum. Earl completed it in 2009.

While he worked on *Grand Isle Diaries,* Earl also monitored a family dispute over the old Thibodeaux property on Bayou Boeuf. The origins of the "unpleasantness" date back to 1960, when approximately twenty-four acres on the west bank held in the name of Novey Rogers, Earl's grandmother, were leased to an oil fabrication company for fifty years at $350 a month. At her death in 1971, the land was willed to her surviving children, and today, nine heirs, including Earl and Eula, own the property jointly. With the original lease closing out in 2010, the heirs, represented by eight attorneys, were discussing, and on bad days arguing, about the land's fate. They couldn't sell it, because to bring the property to EPA standards after fifty years' use by the petroleum industry would cost too much. And so, the central issues included a new lease to an oil-related business and an accurate survey, along with other attendant conditions to be negotiated among the relatives. In conversations with Earl, I've tried to understand and delineate the various agendas and personalities, but I always lose track and throw up my hands, grateful I'm not from a large French family. What I do grasp is that the going rate for the land today, according to Earl, is much better than $350 a month, and if everyone can finally come to an agreement, he and Eula will be able to supplement their government assistance. Earl calls the situation "a nightmare, but with a direction."

Once a resolution is achieved, Earl hopes to hire a carpenter to construct the bookcases he needs, and a handyman to clean out the old brick planters in front of his house and put in some hardy perennials. Most important, though, is a new portable Nagra recorder. The original still needs repairs, and it's too heavy for him to lug around anyway, because of his equilibrium problems. Together with an outboard mixer/phantom power for the Pearl microphone, his current field pack weighs forty-five pounds.

"The Grand Isle project involved going into houses that are built eighteen feet above the ground, and higher," he says. "It was tough getting equipment into houses like that."

I considered the situation for a moment. "Earl," I said, "It looks like the future of your documentary work depends on allowing some arm of the oil industry to continue trashing your family property. How do you feel about that?"

"It's a catch twenty-two," he said.

The land deal continued to drag on through New Year's. In January 2010 Earl, distraught with family tension and worn down with caregiving, sought out a psychiatrist, who offered to put him in the hospital for a few weeks, as a respite. Eula would be taken to an assisted-living facility for the duration. But when the doctor refused to promise that Eula would return to Robicheaux Street when Earl did, Earl called the whole deal off. Instead, he accepted stronger antidepressants and regular sessions with a therapist.

"I guess I'm like a character in a Walker Percy novel," Earl says. "Alive and always on the edge."

. . .

One morning in February 2010, Earl, Randy Dooley, and I met LDWF biologist supervisor Cassidy LeJeune, an Abbeville native, at the Berwick public launch and boarded an official boat to tour the new Atchafalaya Delta. Earl and Randy had looked forward to this trip for weeks; they hadn't plied the bay's waters together since the biology class trip nearly forty years ago, and neither had been out there much since the new delta began to take shape after the 1973 flood. "This is historic," Randy said, rubbing his hands together. "Can you believe we're doing this?" Earl laughed tentatively in agreement. He was concerned about his balance; it had been bothering him more than usual, and his doctor hadn't been able to detect the cause, other than the brain lesions, which hadn't changed. But he had managed to step into the boat and claim a good seat in the cabin, and as we moved out into the bay, Earl and Randy, suited up in winter jackets and life vests, searched the main channel's banks for familiar landmarks, questioning Cassidy: "Where is Pointe au Fer Island? How far is the Wax Lake Delta?" Everything, including the cuts and canals splicing into the river, had changed. Even the cypresses were mostly gone—a few stragglers grasped the west bank, pitched toward the water.

Cassidy, a tall, slender, clear-spoken fellow born after the 1973 flood, obviously enjoyed orienting his elders, steering us farther and farther out into the freshwater bay, identifying the scattered, distant ridges as the emerging delta. All of us knew the delta's aerial map: it looked like an elongated paw print, pointing out to sea. But as Cassidy navigated us through the pads and claws created from naturally accumulated silt and the Army Corps' dredging spoils, we lost all sense of pattern, and the closer to delta land we drew, the more confused we became. Soon Cassidy steered right by Big Island into Breaux Cut and veered left into another, narrower cut, where the land on both banks was signed: Atchafalaya Wildlife Management Area. A campground with picnic tables rolled into view, and farther down, we saw a boat shed for LDWF craft, and staff headquarters set on the hill behind it. Clueless about our position, we'd nevertheless arrived on the paw pad making the deepest impression in the delta.

Inside the headquarters, a spare, clean office and bunkhouse stocked with water, soda, and several months' supply of chips and snack cakes, Cassidy pointed out the delta's features on a large USGS map. The Atchafalaya Delta is part of the Atchafalaya Delta Wildlife Management Area, bordered on the west by the Marsh Island Refuge (west of the Wax Lake Delta) and on the east by Pointe au Fer. Its 137,000 acres include open water, tidal mudflats, aquatic vegetation, emerging vegetation, and uplands—all in transitory states. The area, leased from the Office of State Lands, is intended for conserving and promoting renewable wildlife and fisheries resources, including habitat development. Hunting, trapping, and fishing are permitted here, and there is even a seasonal bow to the old basin houseboat communities—along another side of Headquarters Island lies a mooring area, where rustic camps, some sided like summer cottages, others slapped together with plywood, float in an undulating line toward the open bay.

The area is restricted, though, because three oil and gas companies have leased rights to territory nearby.

"They work with the state to drill as environmentally soundly as possible," Cassidy told us, adding that proceeds from the oil and gas leases go to the state's general fund. The Atchafalaya WMA is supported by that fund, but it does not necessarily receive what's earned within its boundaries. What a WMA receives depends on the conditions set when the leases were granted.

It seemed the paw print was an extension of the big one upstream.

A few minutes later, Earl, Randy, and I were standing by the boat shed, watching Cassidy rev up a large insect of an airboat to give us an even closer look at the delta lands. "It's the only way to see what's happening out there," Cassidy said. "Anyone ever been on one of these?" I had, years ago, in the Everglades, before anyone took many safety precautions, and I might have lost a few scintillas of hearing then from the thwackity roar drilling my ears. The LDWF's airboat carried no fewer than six warning signs: wear a life vest, some eye protection, hearing protection, safety toe footwear, a hard hat, and above all, don't smoke. Earl, Randy, and I donned noise-canceling headphones and waited next to a patch of marsh for Cassidy to run the boat over the headquarters lawn and scoop us up. We hopped in fast, as if catching an amusement park ride in motion, and off we sailed, jerking and bumping over tall, thick cutgrass beds the color of wheat onto a brackish path to the bay. Rounding a bend, we cried out when a surprised doe leapt away and bounced off onto a circle of new terrain.

Once we were in enough water to float and cruise, Cassidy steered us among dots and swatches of land in different stages of development.

Here, within arm's reach, was golden marsh, a few feet away were choco-
laty mudflats, and across a short span of water we saw built-up ridges
sporting winter-thin but tenacious trees planted only a few years before.
"To date, we have built twenty-two thousand acres of marsh habitat,"
Cassidy told us.

"But look what we have lost to gain it," Earl said. "Ironic, isn't it,
that the area of greatest land increase is right next to the area of greatest
loss," he added, looking east in the direction of Grand Isle. We'd just
discussed recent proposals to move silt from the Mississippi Delta into
areas that need it. Critics claim it's too late to mount such an effort. The
story continues.

Cassidy kicked up the airboat's motor, and we zoomed around some
more, savoring the vivid blue sky and the sun's flat heat on our caps and
life vests. The long winter had been getting to all of us; we desperately
needed spring. Driving down from Texas this time, I'd tuned into a radio
station near Lafayette and listened to a deejay rail against global warm-
ing. It was a hoax, the man shouted. How could the earth be heating up
when south Louisiana temperatures were still dropping to the thirties at
night? It was all Al Gore's fault, too. I'd switched stations.

After a while, Cassidy headed us back into marshland and stopped
again, lodging the airboat between two grass islands and turning off the
motor so we could float in relative silence. Against the throaty exhale of
a nearby oil and gas operation, ducks and gulls honked and bleated in
flight, reminding me, oddly, of an urgent little Bach cantata duet I love,
soprano and mezzo playing tag over a rocking cello, clinkity harpsichord,
and fluty pipe organ. Randy asked questions about land management, and
Cassidy explained that everyone with interests here aims to be faithful,
cooperative stewards of the land and water. Earl didn't say anything, indicating polite disagreement. I smiled at Cassidy, because I still believe that
most people are doing the best they know how with the information they
have and the jobs they're charged to do. It's just that the environmental
advocate's wish to encourage choosing the earth's health over personal
or corporate profit feels, some days, like trying to change a ship's course

with a feather. I remind myself that it's a gradual process, part of the life cycle in which we are all participants, not rulers. One day, Grand Isle will sink. One day, the Mississippi will top its levees and hightail it to the sea along a route it chooses. People will adjust—we will change the ways we live, following the old-timers in the basin.

There we sat, rocking.

Back at the Berwick boat launch, Earl, Randy, and I thanked Cassidy LeJeune and debated about where to eat a late lunch. All the local seafood restaurants would be finished with midday service by now, and we had no choice but to drive out to Tampico's on U.S. 90 for chain Mexican food. Inside, a waitress with a local accent seated us at a large table right in the middle of the dining area, from where we could see and hear other patrons: a young family of five, weary from shopping at Walmart, begging for a toddler chair and three peanut butter sandwiches; a retired couple, sunburned, a little testy, just off a swamp tour and wanting margaritas; a pair of middle-aged men in muddy camouflage, gulping Bud Lite with a mound of beef and cheese nachos and not talking; a single woman, middle-aged, dipping her spoon into a bowl of black bean soup, her brow furrowed over a dog-eared copy of Walker Percy's *Lost in the Cosmos*.

The chips at Tampico's were greasy and the salsa too sweet, yet Earl, Randy, and I hung out a full four hours, eating, talking, watching tables fill, clear, fill, and clear again. Somehow, our coffee remained fresh. No one asked us to leave.

I don't recall our conversation in detail, though it had to do with everything that's been written here. Good and important stories deserve retellings, as long as people will remember them. The greatest pleasure that afternoon was the freedom to stay as long as we wanted.

Epilogue

MAY 2010

Fewer than three months after the trip to the Atchafalaya Delta, I was back on Robicheaux Street with Earl and Eula, indulging in what Earl dubbed the Last Suppers. One evening we slurped enormous bowls of Gulf shrimp gumbo, prepared by a new health-care assistant, the first to earn Eula's respect as a cook. Another evening, we gorged ourselves on étouffée of crawfish harvested in a neighborhood bayou. Between meals, we snacked on fresh-shucked oysters dripping with sweet, salty brine, without so much as a cracker to edge out the succulence.

But our mood was not celebratory.

"It might be a long time before we can afford our seafood again," Earl said, reaching for the paper towels, mopping Eula's placemat. "Better enjoy it now."

I couldn't reply to my friend. My mouth was too full, and besides, the moment invited silence. Since the evening of April 20 when an explosion on the Deepwater Horizon, an oil rig off the Louisiana coast leased to petroleum giant BP, triggered the worst environmental disaster in U.S. history, we and so many others had been in mourning. It seemed Louisiana would bear the brunt of this catastrophic event—not a one-time oil spill but an uncontrollable gusher almost impossible to contain. The Pelican State's peerless food supply had almost instantly diminished, crippling the fishing families that had plied the Gulf's waters for generations.

And the pelicans themselves were drowning in oil and chemical dispersants, despite heroic efforts by TriState Bird Rescue and Research, the International Bird Rescue Research Center, the U.S. Fish and Wildlife Service, and scores of volunteers. The brown pelican, the very species pictured on the Louisiana state flag, was particularly vulnerable. Once as familiar along the coast as mockingbirds upcountry, the brown pelicans vanished in the early 1960s after pesticides thinned their eggshells. When adult birds sat on them, they cracked. But after DDT was outlawed in 1972, the birds made a comeback in Louisiana assisted by pairs brought in from a small Florida colony, and in 2009 the brown pelicans were removed from the endangered species list. Now, in 2010, they had been hit by another toxin and were again fighting for their lives on several fronts. For besides weighing down a bird and grounding or drowning it, oil can contaminate its food, penetrate its eggs, and interfere with its ability to regulate body temperature.

"What hasn't been poisoned here?" I said to Earl. "Birds, fish, *you . . .*"

"Now you know why I can't stand the Shrimp and Petroleum Festival," he said.

When I first heard about the festival, it sounded so absurd I could only laugh. The Deep South is famous for weird juxtapositions, and this was just another one. Yet silly pairings often disguise—or in this case, fail to disguise—significant partnerships. Once called simply the Louisiana Shrimp Festival, Morgan City's annual bash was renamed in the 1940s, when Kerr-McGee Industries drilled the first successful offshore oil well out of sight of land, transforming the local economy almost overnight. Even if you can't see the distant derricks or walk the fabrication yards and pipelines lining the river and nearby canals, a glance at the area's billboards touting attorneys specializing in industrial accidents will tell you who's hiring in the community.

And it's not as if families choose either seafood or oil; so many depend on both. During off-season, a fisherman may go to work on a rig. The bookkeeper for a shrimp-packing plant may be married to the foreman on a fabrication site. And so on. In the festival's official logo, a giant shrimp wearing a hard hat curls around an offshore rig, looking out to sea. Morgan City got it right: the delicate crustacean and the tower, named for a type of gallows, are intertwined. And though Earl and others find the image especially distasteful now, it represents a long-term marriage that, without extraordinary measures, can't be dissolved any easier than the oil fouling the ocean's surface, water column, and floor.

.   .   .   .

At the moment, the Atchafalaya Basin is safe, because the spring high water running fast into the bay deters possible pollutants drifting in from the Gulf. Wind and weather are pushing the oil north and east, too. But when the high water subsides, the bay and its marshes will be more vulnerable—and who knows how hurricane season will affect the oil's creep to the shore. Earl's beloved Grand Isle is already ringed with tar, and lower Plaquemines Parish and Barataria Bay are clogged with oil and dispersant.

I asked Wes Tunnell, a biologist with the Harte Research Institute for Gulf of Mexico Studies (Texas A&M–Corpus Christi) and an expert on the 1979 Ixtoc I spill, about the oil's impact on land, and he said that within two to three years, the beaches will clean themselves and the animal life will return to normal. The salt marshes, however, will take decades. Using NOAA's Environmental Sensitivity Index, Tunnell indicated that the marshes rate a ten on a ten-point scale. That is, they're the most vulnerable, and now, they're the most significantly damaged for the long term. "We can't do anything about it," he said. "Eventually the oil in the marshes will start evaporating, leaving something that looks like asphalt. We just have to let nature take its course."

If there is any luck embedded in the BP debacle, it's Earl's timing with the *Grand Isle Diaries*. The fabled barrier island faces possible ruin far sooner than anyone could have predicted in 2009.

. . .

After the Last Suppers, I drove over to New Orleans to speak with Riki Ott, marine toxicologist, community activist, and author of two books on the *Exxon Valdez* spill.

Ott had already been in town for several weeks, assisting community response groups. Besides the ongoing environmental problems Louisiana and the other Gulf states will face, she warned of the social trauma sure to visit shoreline residents, possibly over a long time.

"What if you can't fish? What if the ground is polluted?" she said. "It creates stress that makes people act in ways they wouldn't, normally. After the *Valdez* spill, Cordova (Alaska) had huge spikes in domestic violence, substance abuse, divorce, and suicide, and it took us five years to realize what was going on and how we needed to work together. That's when we started channeling that energy into action."

South Louisiana established community post-trauma networks in 2005 after Hurricane Katrina. Though the BP debacle will severely test them, at least, said Ott, there is someone to sue.

"This is not just an environmental disaster—it's a human rights disaster, too," Ott declared, invoking the EPA's Environmental Justice policy, which defines environmental justice as "fair treatment and meaningful involvement of all people—regardless of race, color, national origin, or income—with respect to development, implementation, and enforcement of environmental laws, regulations, and policies."

Said Ott, "Can we use this policy to declare that the BP spill is an affront on human rights, and push back on the whole oil industry? It's about more than the dollar value of shrimp lost this year or oysters next year—it's the value of maintaining your culture. Yes, some things change with each generation, but you have core values, and you pass them on.

"This area is *home* to people."

* * *

A few days later I was once again in Berwick, driving the bayou roads with Earl. The media frenzy had been getting to him; he'd been hiding out in his room, listening to Bach's B Minor Mass on YouTube, wondering if the spill would be contained by his fifty-sixth birthday in August. It was high time, he said, to get outdoors on a sunny day and take in familiar sights: a snowy egret posing among reeds, a box turtle rocking its way across a dirt lane.

"You know, I'm tired of the reporters who swoop in and say they know what it's like down here," Earl said. "Never before has a culture been so misunderstood. We live off the land and give back to the land. We live in the moment, with the understanding that life is passing. We know we are part of a larger whole.

"People think a crab is isolated, and an oyster is isolated, but that's not so—they are interrelated through smaller organisms. Scientists know this; but some people won't admit it's true, because they need to believe one thing is entirely separate from another. Why? Because that makes it easier to think you can control everything. So you get massive ignorance about the life cycle of an entire ecosystem, and the increased chance that human acts—greedy acts—could bring it down."

I nodded, remembering how a watery ecosystem nourished me

through my Florida childhood, as if I were a little fish egg, swaying in the marsh. Water's links to conception, gestation, and the dream world that coexists with the waking one were as clear as the tide pools I peered into along the Atlantic beach, searching for darting, playful signs of life. Many of us preserve this deep creative connection through access to a pure water source: an ocean, a river, a lake, a neighborhood creek. We have trusted water, relied on it—it is the wellspring of our imagination, the fluency of our flesh. Now, besides grieving the effects of fouled water on the physical health of living things, some of us fear for the health of our souls. How can we live without safe harbor for our spirits, our visions?

·   ·   ·

I continued to ponder the question as Earl and I turned down another road, and the only answer I could think of was the one Earl had given me again and again over the previous five years when I called him on the phone.

"Hey Earl," I say. "How are things?"

"Well—," he says, and pauses, considering, as if he might come up with something different this time.

But he doesn't. On this matter, he is entirely consistent.

"Well, Ann," he says, "I'm still here."

Index

OTHER TITLES IN THE GULF COAST BOOKS SERIES:

Soundfield recordings made on a Nagra IV-S
(Kudelinski) field recorder using an Audio Technica 825
stereo field microphone (XY configuration)
Earl Robicheaux, Soundfield recordist,
mixing supervisor Ivan Klisanin, sound engineer
Recorded December 2, 2003, Lafayette, Louisiana

Atchafalaya Soundscapes
is dedicated to the memory
of Adam Robicheaux